To
Mal Gricken

Best wishes

[signature]

A Million Miles
Over Kansas City

A Million Miles Over Kansas City

The story of John Wagner,
most colorful, controversial, daring,
and certainly the best flying traffic reporter
and street news reporter
in the history of Kansas City broadcasting

By

CHARLES GRAY

Leathers Publishing
A division of Squire Publishers, Inc.
4500 College Blvd.
Leawood, KS 66211
1/888/888-7696

ISBN: 1-58597-040-9

A division of Squire Publishers, Inc.
4500 College Blvd.
Leawood, KS 66211
1/888/888-7696

FOREWORD

THE NEWS BUSINESS has always been populated by colorful characters, none more so than the small band prowling the streets of Kansas City when I arrived in town in the middle of the twentieth century.

These men gathered the material that enhanced what journalists wrote. Their exploits, with their own style of news gathering, were every bit as colorful as the people and events they covered, often even more so.

They included: Sol Studna, Brooks Crummit, Roger Reynolds and Joe Wellington of the *Kansas City Star and Times;* Wes Lyle of United Press International; Bill Straeter of Associated Press; Sam Feeback, Ted Rice, Joe Adams, Montie Finnell, Marshall Brown, Leroy Scott, Phil French and Richard Herrera, of television channels four, five and nine, and John Wagner, who spent his Kansas City broadcast news years at KMBC (later KMBZ) and then with WDAF Radio. He is the only radio man on the list.

While this volume centers on John Wagner, it is also intended as a tribute to the other members of that special brotherhood of street newsmen, whose work made life so interesting, and whose energy and enthusiasm made it difficult to keep up with them, and all but impossible to beat them.

They got out from behind desks and went out onto the streets to experience rain, snow, tornadoes, floods, gunfire, and yes, danger. They got wet, hot, cold, dirty, and they also got the news. They went "out there" because that's where the news is.

They don't make many like them any more. And that's too bad.

Charles Gray

INTRODUCTION

... 7:05 ON A SPRING MORNING in 1987. A Kansas City man had just completed breakfast at an east-side diner. It was a daily stop, almost automatic. It was so routine the man hardly remembers getting into his car and heading it toward the street.

He was barely listening to the car radio which was always set at 610, WDAF, because he liked cowboy music and the station's dedication to breaking news and traffic problems.

Suddenly, a mournful cowboy song ended, and the pace changed with a very excited flying traffic reporter. He and his airplane were above a high-speed chase in Jackson County.

The man stopped the car before entering the street. Just then the airborne traffic reporter began calling out the color and description of the car and where it was headed, with police in pursuit at speeds of 80, 85, 90 miles an hour. Then the reporter named the street our listener was about to enter. He was paying close attention now. At that instant the speeding procession zipped past him.

He would have been right in the path, had he not been listening to that radio station. Realizing he had just had a very close call, he felt he had to let WDAF know what it had done for him.

He wrote a letter, declaring, "John Wagner saved my life"

The Greater Kansas City Safety Council learned of it, and at an annual awards luncheon presented John a special citation.

John was flattered, of course, and grateful for the recognition. But car chases were nothing new in his exciting life. Neither were tornadoes, explosions, gun battles, bank robberies, five-alarm fires or hostage seizures. He loved emergencies as long as he could be in the middle of them.

They make up much of the story of his exciting life.

Chapter 1

IN THE BEGINNING ...

JOHN DAVID WAGNER arrived on this earth, kicking and screaming, squalling and brawling, in Chicago, May 19, 1928. His mother was Alice. John has no memory of her. She left in a divorce while he was still a baby. His father's name was Leslie.

John and his sister were raised by their grandparents in a north-side apartment. His dad also lived there, but left the child-rearing to the grandparents. Grandmother was the family matriarch.

John's early years were spent as a student in St. Henry's Catholic School. Along with school he remembers running, skipping, climbing trees, and all the things happy little boys love to do.

He also remembers that classes were taught and the "law" was enforced by nuns. One particularly fearsome nun was Sister Rigaberta, who frequently thumped John sharply on the back of the head with a sewing thimble. On occasion he was forced to hold out his hands, while the nun whacked him across the knuckles with a three-sided ruler.

As he was to do often later in life, John pushed the limits with Sister Rigaberta (whose name behind her back was Rigor Mortis). One day the nun took John by the ear and pulled him to the front of the class and gave him a stern lecture. "If you don't stop talking, young man, you'll never amount to anything." Little did she know what a talkative life he was to live.

John never resented the harsh discipline. "It helped to mold me. You learned that when the Sisters told you to do or not do something, that was it. There was no Court of Appeals. In fact, trouble at school often meant even more serious trouble at home in the form of a whuppin."

Many years later in his adult life, when John was briefly out of broadcasting, he managed movie theaters in Kansas City and was in charge of hiring and firing personnel. He used the Sisters' approach to dealing with errant human beings (minus the physical aspects). The nuns in Chicago never knew that their teaching was passed along to rookie theater ushers in the form of shined shoes, polished uniform buttons, clean shirts, neckties and well-combed hair.

"Those nuns whacked us, but they never took away our pride. They saw to it that we took pride in doing what they told us."

After school John was part of a group of about 10 boys who lived in the neighborhood. They played games, swam together in Lake Michigan, spent time on girls' front porches, rode in a pal's 1934 Ford.

"We never got into serious trouble ... never committed any crimes, unless you consider it criminal to climb the high scaffolding on a coalyard and throw pieces of coal down on the others below, and occasionally onto a passing train. For us it was fun, for the coalyard watchmen, it was something else.

"We never broke the law or got into trouble with the police. If the police should ever call the house to complain, I can well imagine what my grandfather would have done with that heavy strap. He used it on me for other offenses, and I remember every one of them."

John's memories of his father are not totally pleasant. He says his dad was never at home during the day because he was out struggling to make a living during the Great Depression. When his father was home was late at night, frequently drunk. John says his father always wanted to drag him out of bed in the middle of the night to engage in a rambling senseless conversation.

One night it was too much. While being led down the long hall to the kitchen on a school night, John recalls protesting and backing that protest with a fist into his father's face. This brought quick retaliation ... a haymaker punch ... the first time John can remember seeing stars.

John never raised a hand against his father again, nor was he ever again dragged from bed in the middle of the night to be forced to talk with a man who had been drinking for hours. "Those are the memories of my father. I wish they had been better."

About that time, during World War II, some of John's slightly older friends were coming home on leave in Army, Navy or Marine Corps uniforms. He wanted to try his hand in the military. He turned 17 in 1945 and learned that if a parent signed a consent form, a young man could get in at that age.

John was not doing well in school, and his relationship with the only parent he knew was not going well either. The elder Wagner signed the form, and John was on his way to Navy boot camp.

John Wagner (right) and a navy buddy taking a break during the war.

John managed to get in on some of the action in the Marianas, Tinian, Saipan, Guam. Duty consisted mainly of guarding small groups of Japanese war prisoners on minor work details. The prisoners were young, some even younger than Seaman Wagner.

On one detail, John called a break, sat down, leaned his rifle against a tree, and promptly dozed off. A sniper shot woke him in a hurry. Worse yet, when his eyes opened, he saw one of his prisoners holding *his* rifle. As Wagner mentally prepared to die, the young prisoner grinned, said, "Here, Joe," tossed the rifle to John, and pointed out where he thought the sniper was. IIe lived through the experience, and thereafter kept a close eye on the prisoner who saved his life.

Though they, the American and the Japanese, didn't speak the same language, they seemed to like each other. In Wagner's words, "It's hard to hate someone who had a chance to kill you, and didn't."

Most of the young Japanese prisoners were barefoot. A lucky few wore flimsy Japanese sandals. His young "friend" let John know how much he admired and coveted the regulation navy shoes his American captors wore.

The Americans, always resourceful, operated an underground economy, tapping into some of the navy's supply stores. Beer was swapped, along with cigarettes, articles of clothing, even some food. John was able to penetrate the system. That ability would come in handy years later, when he was a street crime reporter in Wichita and Kansas City.

The atomic bombs fell on Hiroshima and then Nagasaki, and the war ended. Ships left daily for Japan, returning the Japanese war prisoners to their homes. When the last one sailed, one of its young passengers was proudly carrying a pair of brand new regulation U.S. Navy shoes (of course, they were coated with mud and made to look old and worn.

Their owner, that young Japanese soldier, already knew what policemen, fireman and other public safety workers would learn years later ... that John Wagner never forgot a favor or a friend. In his words, "There's always a tomorrow."

Seaman John Wagner on Tinian during final months of world war two

As the Japanese prisoners headed home, the Americans realized that their time on the islands was to end pretty soon. And in time John Wagner found himself back on Chicago's north side.

But it wasn't the same. He had been to war, considered himself a "man of the world," and found the company of his younger friends who didn't go to war, boring.

He summed it all up. He had been in the Navy one year, 11 months, 21 days and 22 minutes ... all without a leave.

A pre-war girlfriend, the pretty figure skater he had met in Chicago, had moved to Wichita, Kansas. And John headed for the Sunflower State.

The romance flowered, bloomed, faded and died.

Despite the great career opportunities promised by a GI bill-financed training course in heating and air conditioning repair, John was not doing well. He moved from job to job, finding little satisfaction or success.

Amid all this John could not foresee the personal life changes and great opportunities that lay ahead. He got a job with Plainview Furniture in a neighborhood not far from McConnell Air Force Base. Business was good in that residential neighborhood, filled with young Air Force and Boeing aircraft families.

The store owner, Nevin Mendenhall, decided to advertise on local radio station KWBB, which broadcast a country music disc jockey show from the store's front window one night a week. Station performers chatted with customers and store employees, among them John Wagner. They discussed special merchandise, the items being featured that week, and it was successful.

One night the man who regularly handled the broadcast for KWBB was ill. The station news director, Jim Setters, urged John to appear on the program himself.

John resisted, saying he had no experience, didn't even know how to "spin" a record. Setters was unmoved. He was a man who believed in getting out into the streets and covering live, dangerous news. A man who stared into gun barrels and got close to burning buildings was not about to be refused by a mere flunky in a furniture store.

A nervous John Wagner soon was in front of the KWBB microphone. And unless history has skipped a few pages, it was the only time John ever shied away from a mike.

On that initial broadcast John veered away from the music and tried his hand at ad-libbing. He was a natural. He was soon yelling at the audience, "You'd better get yourself down here to Plainview Furniture. You know where it is. You know we're the best ... get down here."

It all went well for quite a while. But in this life nothing is permanent. Business trends changed, and for business reasons Mr. Mendenhall closed the Plainview store and moved downtown to the central Wichita business district. John didn't make the move.

John had made some contacts with the appliance business while working at Plainview Furniture. He soon found work with Model Kitchen, a firm specializing in everything to do with kitchens ... floors, cabinets, counters and appliances. This was fateful.

His work at Model Kitchen put John in contact with Siebert and Willis, an appliance wholesaler.

On one of John's visits to the wholesaler, an attractive young lady in the bookkeeping department caught his attention. Despite all his efforts, and there were many, she never agreed to go out with him.

Failing to impress the first young lady, John noticed one of her co-workers. She was even more attractive. Helen Vanderbeke didn't care much for Wagner at first. "He was cocky, smart aleck and pushy."

Of course he was. He was John Wagner.

Eventually Helen Vanderbeke agreed to go out with John. His persistence paid off. In early September 1955 John and Helen were married.

A year later Jimmy was born. And a couple of years after that, daughter Terri was born.

The Model Kitchen job didn't last forever. End of furniture and appliance career.

John found work at a dry cleaner shop making pickups and deliveries in the company truck. His earlier chance encounter with Jim Setters, the radio news director, was fateful. Though he didn't know it, John's life was making a big turn. He began to "run" with Setters. He spent his spare time riding with Setters in the radio station's Oldsmobile 88 news car. It was equipped with all kinds of radio equipment. John was fascinated. He liked the idea of communicating from the field by radio, he liked Setters, he liked radio, and he loved the excitement of a fire, a car crash, a bank robbery or a rescue from floodwaters. He was not destined to spend the rest of his life in a dry cleaner's truck.

Among the equipment in the radio news car were two old surplus radio receivers, used years earlier on Boston streetcars and later sold through radio equipment surplus houses.

Setters suggested that John take one of these and hide it on his dry cleaner truck, so the radio station could reach him by sounding a tone. The tone alerted John to call the radio station by phone and learn where he was to go to cover a breaking news story for the radio station, all the while on the dry cleaner payroll.

In John Wagner's words: "As I would drive around Wichita in that truck, I would listen to KWBB. Now, Setters knew roughly what part of town I would be in at a given time." He said Setters would break in on a regular radio program with a report on a breaking news story ... saying, "We are watching a house fire at such and such an address, and if we're lucky, we'll have a reporter there shortly for a live report."

That was John's cue. He would hurry to the fire scene and call the radio station by telephone. He didn't claim to be a reporter. The radio news director would tell John to explain merely what he could see ... in other words, "Let your eyes tell the story." The KWBB newsroom taped the report, edited it and used it later on a regular newscast.

This presented a problem. The radio station claimed it had no money to pay John. He had to be careful. If the dry cleaner caught him, he would lose the job he needed so badly. To mask his identity, he referred to himself as "Unit X."

Chapter 2

A NEW CAREER IN WICHITA

JOHN WAGNER'S "double life" was to come to an end. The mysterious Unit X was unmasked on a day the Air Force was celebrating the graduation of the 1000th B-47 pilot from the flight training school at McConnell Air Force Base. The high point of the celebration was a flyover of 300 B-47 jet bombers, which were built at the Boeing aircraft plant at Wichita.

The event attracted *Life Magazine* and aviation writers from scores of publications all over the country to Wichita. To accommodate the reporters, the Air Force provided a World War II vintage B-25 bomber as a chase plane to carry them within camera range of the jet bombers.

The fact that he was being paid by the dry cleaner shop didn't keep John from covering this big story ... from that B-25 chase plane. The radio station arranged to get one of its radio rigs aboard the press plane, and John Wagner, alias Unit X, was in business and doing what was to be his first airborne radio broadcast. It was a heady experience. He was jammed into a jump seat behind pilot and co-pilot. When the B-25 was airborne, the co-pilot climbed out of his right side seat and told John to move in. "It was great," John recalls. "I could see everything and could hear much of the noise, and this was all going on the radio."

All went well until the control tower told the B-25 pilot he had a very brief window to land, between the hundreds of jets, and would have to hurry. The pilot told John to get out of the right side seat and put the plane in a steep angle for landing … John didn't quite make it out of his temporary cockpit seat.

The old twin-engined bomber descended at a faster rate than the contents of John's stomach. In his words, that cockpit was a mess. When that plane rolled to a stop, "I was white as a white shirt … and smelled to high heaven."

When I got back to the dry cleaner truck which had been out in the sun all day, I tried to clean up, but I was as sick as a dog." "I drove it back to the dry cleaner shop and was so sick I was nearly staggering. My boss came over and asked if I was sick. When I told him I had an upset stomach, he said maybe you ought to go back to that airplane and find it. He had heard the broadcast, said it was fantastic and, incidentally, you're fired."

End of dry cleaning career.

John Wagner's radio career had a rocky beginning. He admits he couldn't read a newscast on the air. His friend Jim Setters tutored and encouraged him. But that part of the news broadcasting business never yielded to John's determination.

Setters had him memorize a script (it took a week). The result was an acceptable demonstration tape. But when faced with deadlines, station management regarded John's newsreading as a disaster.

Then Setters had another idea. Since John could do well out in the field, why not try him there as an outside mobile news reporter?

John recalls: "You name it … I covered it. I covered everything from hatchet murders to tornadoes … even caught a couple of them." Covered every kind of fire you ever imagined … from high rise to single family homes to trailers … covered them all."

John felt he owed the station management a debt for sticking with him and giving him a job when he lost his other one. He worked many extra hours to justify the $47 a week the radio station was paying him.

"Wichita may not sound like much, he says, but let me tell you a lot of news is generated there."

Something else generated in Wichita was John Wagner's ability to deal with hostile, domineering personalities.

One was Joe Klepper, Wichita Police Department detective. He seemed to enjoy being rude to reporters and delighted in slamming his office door just as John approached.

John was not exactly Dale Carnegie himself, but he managed to find an opening to Joe Klepper. He learned that the harsh, gruff, unreasonable Joe Klepper was a Boy Scout leader.

On his next approach to the Klepper office, and just as the door was slammed in his face, John caught it and pushed it open. And standing chin to chin with the much larger detective, John snarled, "Is that what you teach your Boy Scouts to do, Klepper, slam the door in somebody's face?"

Caught off guard, Klepper replied, "How did you find that out?"

John quickly assured him he had his own sources of information, and besides, he promised to protect Klepper's secret … that he was really a pretty decent fellow, something Klepper didn't want out on the street. Another tough nut to crack was Wichita's new Chief of Police. Gene Pond had been an FBI agent, then chief of the detective bureau of the Kansas City Police Department, then was hired by Wichita.

Pond, a wiry, grim-faced man with steely blue eyes that could drill holes through a hoodlum lying to him, was strictly in the mold of a J. Edgar Hoover G-man … see all, hear all, absorb all, and tell nothing. Gene Pond was also one of the best policemen who ever lived.

John quickly learned that he and Pond shared some traits. They both liked to be first at the scene of whatever was happening, and they both believed that going anywhere at less than 90 miles an hour was too slow.

What emerged from the "bridge building" with those two very hard-nosed characters is best described as respect, if not total friendship.

From those relationships came even closer contact with the officers on the street. They genuinely liked John, admired his spunk and helped him whenever they could.

In the next few years John became even better established as the voice of radio news on the streets of Wichita. He did this by being where things were happening. That, of course, required some innovation and daring. One day while John was at Police Headquarters he heard that a bomb had been detonated at Wichita International Airport. John left by one door, and Police Chief Pond left by another. At speeds reaching 90 miles an hour, the two arrived at the blast scene seconds apart … Pond just ahead.

When Pond saw Wagner, he asked, "What kept you?" That let Wagner know he and Pond could work together.

That story and others helped cement what was to become the Wagner philosophy that the best way to cover news for radio was from inside … to be so close the listener could hear not just the reporter, but the sounds of the story itself … the crackle of flames, the sound of brick walls falling, the rush of floodwaters, actual gunshots … in effect, "the sound of things."

Though it involved some personal risk, it became John's trademark.

This required some different equipment. The standard reporter notepad and pencil are hardly adequate for radio news. Engineers rigged a portable transmitter for John. The car battery that powered it was so heavy, it had to be rolled along on a two-wheel cart. It slowed a usually fleet-footed reporter, but good ideas have to start somewhere.

A big grain elevator fire several miles outside Wichita was the testing ground for the new radio rig. Pulling the heavy "trailer," John went into the elevator at its base and noted that the only way to get to the top was to ride a man lift … a conveyor belt device that is equipped with folding steps and grip bars. Riding one of them is tricky business and requires experience and caution.

Being inexperienced and having little use for caution, John rode the lift to the top, broadcast live back to Wichita until his radio battery ran down, and remounted the lift to ride it down. He didn't jump off in time and ended up in the pit. It was completely dark and filled with grain dust. It took some ingenuity to get out of that, but he did. He felt for the grip in the dark, grabbed it and rode up until he saw daylight and jumped clear.

His next Wichita adventure involved a fire at a grease company tank farm near downtown. He and the entire fire department were there.

John noticed that a fireman with a high pressure hose was atop a very tall and fat tank. In seconds he was up there with the fireman ... thanks to a steel ladder stair. Radio listeners heard the fireman's name, and how he was doing up there shooting water at nearby burning tanks. Almost as an aside, Wagner asked what was in the tank beneath him. When the fireman told him it was a highly explosive product, John quickly decided to find another vantage point.

The engineering technicians at the Wichita radio station were very helpful to John, and to the business of getting exciting news on the air live. They made a 50-foot microphone cord for the portable transmitter, for those times when it was better to use the electric power from the car.

John used it for the first time in a nightclub fire. He parked as close as he could ... connected the cord to the car radio unit, threw the other end of the cord into the window. Then, carrying the microphone, he ran into the building from the other side, connected the microphone and let his audience hear what it was like inside a burning building while it was happening!

A tornado hit El Dorado, a town northeast of Wichita. Confident that all the state troopers were dealing with the storm and too busy to arrest a speeding newsman, John got there in half an hour.

The range was not quite right. A radio signal could barely reach Wichita from ground level. No problem. Engineers from the radio station hurried to the storm-stricken city, hung a temporary antenna cable from a water tower, and Wichita radio listeners miles away got the story from the man who, it seemed, was always there.

Taking the chances, testing the limits and exploring new ways of getting live news on the radio were battle-tested in Wichita. And they would soon be refined and pushed to another level in a larger city.

But despite all that, the Wichita days were nearing an end. John recalls going in to see the station manager to seek a raise and being told he had already reached the salary limit for his work … good as it was by then.

With fate always at his side, John was told that a Kansas City radio salesman, turned consultant, was in town, was at a local motel and wanted to talk with him.

As John later learned, the salesman, Johnny Pearson, had listened extensively to KWBB and picked up more ideas on radio news coverage than he brought with him.

A major news story interrupted John's plan to call the visitor, and they never talked until much later. Meanwhile Pearson returned to Kansas City with stories of exciting local news coverage he had heard in Wichita … a city where radio listeners heard a radio reporter go to robberies, crashes, fires, explosions and report live what he was seeing, and talking to people who were involved in the stories.

Eventually KMBC sent another man to Wichita, and he made direct contact with John Wagner … and a deal was made.

But before John got away from Wichita, he had to say good-bye to the many friends he had cultivated among his news sources. Many of them were sheriffs, police chiefs, cops on the street, fire chiefs and firemen on the rigs, store clerks, cab drivers, tow truck operators, judges, city officials and many others.

The City Commission called a special meeting … and City Manager Frank Backstrom, an old city government pro from Kansas City, handed John an inscribed City Commission resolution thanking him for his service to Wichita as a broadcast reporter. And along with the resolution came a letter of introduction to H. Roe Bartle, the colorful mayor of Kansas City, Missouri. The Wichita City Commission made no note in its resolution of John's service to the furniture or dry cleaning industry in Wichita.

End of Wichita phase of the John Wagner career.

Resolution

NOW, THEREFORE, BE IT RESOLVED that the Board of City Commissioners does hereby recognize and commend John D. Wagner for his outstanding coverage of city news by radio to the citizens of Wichita during the past seven years and express our best wishes for his continued success on behalf of the City Commission, the City Manager and his staff, other news media representatives, and the city and citizens of Wichita.

BE IT FURTHER RESOLVED as gesture of the high regard and esteem in which he is held, that the Clerk of the City be instructed to spread a copy of this resolution in the permanent records of the City of Wichita.

ADOPTED at Wichita, Kansas, this _12th_ day of _February_, 1963.

Carl A. Bell

Carl A. Bell, Jr.
Mayor

Attest:

C. H. Funk

C. H. Funk
City Clerk

15

Chapter 3

ON TO KANSAS CITY ...

JOHN, HELEN and the two children arrived in Kansas City in February 1963, not knowing exactly what lay ahead.

Kansas City was bigger than Wichita, where Helen grew up, but smaller than Chicago, where John grew up. Despite its size, it was still a strange city. And a broadcast street reporter can't do his job unless he knows the place.

For the average newcomer, Greater Kansas City can be a challenge. It touches parts of two states, three counties in Kansas and four in Missouri. The list of municipalities is endless, the biggest, of course, are Kansas City, Missouri, and Kansas City, Kansas.

Add to that the fact that the numbered streets on the Missouri side run east and west and in Kansas City, Kansas (always a different place), they run north and south. But John Wagner was not about to be intimidated by the geographic maze.

He had always been an innovator and a quick study ... traits that have served him well all his life.

Armed with a printed street guide for Greater Kansas City (circa 1963) and the big black Mercury sedan KMBC provided, John set out to "learn" Kansas City.

He drove the streets by day and by night. He says night driving is the best learning method. "Night sights, with the electric marquees, street lights and traffic signals, combined with the network of alleys, building shapes and other charac-

IMMEDIATE RELEASE FROM ...

"TO KEEP IN TOUCH WITH THE TIMES

... keep tuned to KMBC Radio News." That's a familiar sound around Kansas City . But John Wagner, new KMBC Mobile Newsman, plans to make it a "household word."

John comes to KMBC from KWBB in Wichita, Kansas. His main job will be to find the news and cover it on the spot for KMBC Radio.

To aid John in his work, his special news unit is equipped with police and fire radios, the KMBC two-way radio, a professional first aid kit, stretcher, fire axe, fire extinguisher, five-gallon can of gasoline, tow chain, jump cables, life preserver, a coil of rope, bag of sand, flares, gas mask, asbestos coat, hat and boots, a heavy-duty flashlight and blankets.

Whether you see John Wagner rushing to cover a big story of simply interviewing the "man of the street," you'll know — "to keep in touch with the times, keep tuned to KMBC Radio News."

THE KANSAS CITY METROPOLITAN BROADCASTING SYSTEM

teristics you don't notice during the day give you the best possible mental picture of a place."

In only a couple of weeks, John could find his way around town better than the average cabbie or ambulance driver. He navigated better even than police officers. They are confined to a specific district. John's "beat" was bigger than any of their patrol zones.

The process of getting to know Kansas City was briefly interrupted by one more emergency in Wichita. An Air Force KC-97 aerial tanker, loaded with thousands of gallons of jet fuel, crashed minutes after taking off from McConnell Air Force Base.

The plane went down in a fireball, leaving a charred crater in a residential neighborhood, killing a number of people including the crew.

The story hit Kansas City quickly. Some of its radio and television stations were trying to "spread their wings" and take on news coverage of a more regional nature.

While some Kansas City radio news directors tried to make telephone contact with anyone in Wichita who would talk to them (the cheapest way to "cover" the story), television news directors dithered over which of their stars to send to Wichita. KMBC realized it had a great double threat weapon. John Wagner was already a seasoned reporter, could learn to shoot a movie camera quickly, and knew Wichita like the back of his hand. It was an easy decision.

The speedometer needle in the big black Mercury sedan was permanently bent that day as Wagner nearly flew to Wichita in Unit Thirteen. He got there in record time, got the initial story covered for KMBC radio, filmed it for KMBC-TV, and managed to secure his station's position at the scene until a regular cameraman from Channel Nine could get there. Knowing the territory paid handsome dividends for KMBC that day.

Being cocky, smart aleck and pushy, as his wife has already described him, may have caused some public relations problems for him along the way but, like it or not, a street

Wagner, covering New Puritan Hotel Fire at 9th and Wyandotte —
downtown Kansas City

reporter without those qualities is wasting his time. The alternative is to go over and stand behind the rope, like a sheep, and wait for those in charge to provide an information "feeding." That's the way the Kansas City Police Department now demands it.

On the day a midtown Kansas City saloon blew up, either by natural gas or at the hands of Mafia land clearance teams, John wanted to go to the explosion. His news director sent him instead to a water main break on Southwest Boulevard. He went to the water problem.

"When I got there, this geyser of water was shooting 25 feet in the air, flooding all low-lying streets. Traffic was blocked in all directions. I waded into the water, farther than I should have, and stuck my mike nearly into the water. On tape it sounded like Niagara Falls. It was such exciting sound, Mark Foster, one of the disc jockeys, played it every half hour the next day."

John doesn't remember how the saloon explosion came out. Neither does anyone else. There's no reason to remember. Wagner didn't cover it.

While John continued to become familiar with the ways of Kansas City, the city's criminals continued to rob and kill other people.

One cold afternoon a couple of holdup men went into a large downtown office building. As they got off the elevator on an upper floor, they pulled on masks, drew their guns and walked into the offices of a wholesale jewelry company. Even though they met no resistance, they handcuffed their victims to a cast iron steam radiator. This gave them time to loot the vault at their leisure. No one would say what the loss was, but unofficial circles later estimated it was at several million dollars.

It was not the perfect crime. The thugs had not counted on a downtown traffic policeman, Arlie Watts, or on his suspicious nature. Watts quickly smelled a rat, took custody of the robbers, and had them at gunpoint when backup officers arrived.

When Watts called for assistance, it alerted not only other police, but also John Wagner, who got there in very short order.

This gave police time to establish a "crime scene" and keep everyone out of the building, to newsman Wagner's great displeasure.

Finally, an "in-charge" looking man in a police uniform came out past the reporters and cameramen. In keeping with his earlier law enforcement career, the man would not answer any questions or give the reporters any information.

John noticed that the man's name tag read Kelley ... and that the man wore silver braid on his cap bill and silver eagles, indicating high rank. It was John's first meeting with Kansas

City's new Police Chief Clarence Kelley, and it was not a cordial encounter.

John radioed a report back to the KMBC Newsroom and asked that it be taped for later use on a newscast. In the report John referred to the man as General Kelley. The news director wouldn't touch it and would not authorize its broadcast.

That refusal led to another face-off between John and his news director. John ran into the manager's office and was told that General Manager Dave Croninger was at the Muehlebach Hotel barbershop two blocks away getting a shave.

The boss, face covered with a hot towel, was horizontal in the barber chair when his peaceful moment was interrupted by an excited Wagner saying: "Dave, we've got a problem."

Abandoning the shave, Croninger walked back to the radio station with his agitated street reporter. They went directly to the newsroom, and John insisted that the manager listen to his tape. When informed what it contained, Croninger turned to the news director and said, "I don't need to hear it. Just put it on the air."

The experience gave John confidence that he would be backed when he needed backing. It was not totally a blank check, and John was reminded that he had to go by the rules.

As a foot note to the robbery story, Clarence Kelley can't be faulted for not talking to newsmen that day. He had just arrived in Kansas City, after 25 years as an FBI agent, and didn't know any of the reporters just yet. His relationship with newsmen later became quite cordial (to the envy of some of Kelley's successors).

Another explanation for Kelley's reluctance to talk that day was the fact that one of the bandits was the son of a police detective, and that's always touchy territory for a police executive.

So it all ended reasonably well. The bad guys went to prison. Downtown traffic officer Arlie Watts was honored for his heroism. The wholesale jewelers got their money and diamonds back. Station manager Dave Croninger finally got his shave. Clarence Kelley was returned to his proper rank …

Colonel or Chief. And everything was as it should be except John Wagner's relationship with his news director.

Those are the hazards of being a cocky, pushy and sometimes smart-aleck street reporter who also happens to be one of the very best in the business.

As time went by, Wagner's range of experience widened, and so did the field of new ideas he was willing to try.

For example, he began to use the sound of sirens while he was still enroute to a breaking story. If he managed to get in behind the fire trucks as they screamed though the city, it was easy. Just put the microphone out the window and do a report on where they were going and what the audience could expect to hear.

This was not always a howling success. He admits that one day he pulled into the caravan of fire trucks and was letting his audience hear the sirens and perhaps believe it might be the fire of the century. With keen embarrassment, John dutifully reported that when the first fire crews got to the fire scene, one man rushed into the apartment building, found the fire source and carried it outside ... (a burning mattress!)

Because of his style and his hustle, John Wagner and Unit Thirteen were warmly welcomed at fire and crime scenes. Firemen and policemen considered him their friend. He often helped them when they needed another pair of hands.

Unit Thirteen was well equipped. On top was a revolving emergency light, fitted with white or clear elements. It had the same effect as modern-day strobe lights. You couldn't miss it!

One night John was rolling behind some fire companies on their way to a big one in the southern part of the city. Down the trafficway, then through the Plaza, and as the convoy headed south on Ward Parkway, John saw the chief's car pull over and stop at 55th Street.

As he drew near, he saw someone waving him over. He approached the "buggy," as they are still called. Battalion Chief Benny Imperiale said, "Your lights are brighter than mine. You lead and I'll follow. You know the address."

So, he recalls, "I led Benny and several of his companies to the fire."

On "slow" news days John would either cruise city streets or go to one of the many vantage points he had chosen about town for quick access to any street if anything happened.

One such day he chose the point, a parking spot on the bluff overlooking the north-south runway on Municipal Airport. It was a raw, blustery day, not at all nice. A small airplane was approaching for a landing and came right over John's head. Suddenly a gust of wind caught the plane, sent it into a loop, crashing in the Missouri River.

On the air in seconds, John was describing the incident and was at the riverbank when the only survivor was pulled from the water. He told John he had mentally practiced kicking the back window out of the plane in event of trouble. He did so and was pulled out of the aircraft by the river current. It saved his life. His fellow passengers didn't make it.

John has always believed in having an escape route, a fallback position or whatever you call it. The story of that plane crash survivor gave further proof to the value of contingency planning.

But not all fall-back positions are foolproof, as John realized in a multi-alarm fire in an old near downtown building, known in its better days as the New Puritan Hotel. Fire was already well advanced in the New Puritan Hotel by the time the first fire companies arrived. The old, near-downtown, six-story building, painted an ugly shade of green, was spewing smoke from several levels, and flame was coming out upper floor windows and the roof.

John Wagner got there just as the situation moved to the second and third-alarm levels. He opened the car trunk and got into the heavy rubber coat with the radio station call-letters painted on the back, the hard hat, the boots, and picked up his newer version walkie talkie. He broadcast a couple of quick reports from outside the building to let KMBC listeners hear what was happening, then headed for the door.

The first fireman he encountered was Charles Fisher, then

a captain. They were friends and east-side neighbors and raised their children together. John called him Chuck.

When Wagner told Fisher he planned to go into the burning building, Fisher said he would go with him, but warned that they must stay close to the walls. The floors were already seriously weakened by the fire. The order was "hug the baseboards."

The two made their way to the second, the third and the fourth floors. Then they separated. Fisher's job was to supervise his company. This left John alone on four.

It was quite a sight ... the old building surrounded on three sides by aerial trucks of all kinds, hook and ladder rigs and a snorkel, which was on John's side of the building. He was having a field day until he noticed that the smoke was getting thicker, the air was getting much hotter, and the floor had sagged about a foot. He got to a window and saw the snorkel platform or basket a floor above. He used the fire escape to climb one floor and scrambled onto the basket. It was a terrific vantage point to broadcast the story.

Then an old problem returned to haunt him. The walkie talkie battery ran down. He told the fireman on the snorkel he would have to go down and get a fresh battery. The fireman was sympathetic, but he couldn't lower the rig. His job was to fight the fire.

John understood and climbed back onto the fire escape and carefully started down. He was just level with the third floor when he heard a grinding noise that worried him. It should have worried him. The fire escape anchor bolts were pulling loose from the damaged building. John was descending what had been a secure stairway, which had become, in effect, a swinging ladder six or seven stories tall.

He made a quick decision to get back inside the building on three, hug the baseboards and find a stairway. It was a good move. He went to Unit Thirteen parked near the building, got a fresh battery and wisely covered the rest of the big story from ground level.

The fire was eventually knocked down. Later the build-

Newsman John getting facts from the man in charge

ing was demolished. John Wagner lived to cover other fires and exciting news stories.

And Charles Fisher went on to become, many years later, Director and Chief of the Kansas City Fire Department. Fisher retired in late 1996 with distinction.

John describes his old friend as "the most responsible and professional fireman I ever knew."

Wagner's words about Fisher were echoed by many others. One paid him the ultimate fireman's compliment: "I always felt safer fighting a fire under Chief Fisher than with any other chief."

In other words, if you were in a fire fight alongside Fisher, you really had to try to get yourself hurt. And despite all of John Wagner's efforts in that direction, he managed to survive scores of major disasters.

Chapter 4

WAGNER GETS HIS WINGS AND MOVES ON

WHILE OJT (on the job training) is not generally recommended in most of aviation, it was John's ticket to a pilot's license.

While riding in the KMBZ helicopter with pilot/instructor each morning, John paid close attention.

When the helicopter flight for broadcast was over, the two would move to a fixed-wing Cessna for some hands-on flight instruction.

At the same time, John was attending ground school and came in second in a class of 93.

When sufficient training hours had been accumulated, John and Henry Langley flew to MCI airport (Mid Continent International Airport) for a final solo effort.

John flew solo twice that stormy day, and afterward was told he was qualified to apply for a pilot's license. Henry signed his logbook.

When John left KMBZ years later, his logbook contained 4,000 flying hours.

When he left WDAF, even later, it bore more than 13,000 hours. That amounts to about one million miles, virtually all flown in a control zone.

Many commercial airline pilots don't have nearly that many hours at the controls.

*MCI, now generally known as KCI (Kansas City International Airport) was under construction in those days. Incidentally, MCI is still its official designation in legal aviation circles.

As John Wagner moved from one dramatic event to another, his style of covering exciting news events continued to develop.

Big fires became one of his specialties. And no more fertile field for spectacular fires could be found than in the area's many aging slaughter houses and meat-packing plants. Kansas City was no longer America's slaughter house. Most of the old plants were closed, victims of new meat-packing techniques. Wrecking crews couldn't get around to them fast enough.

This left many big, old and very combustible buildings idle. Most were cork-lined for insulation purposes, and the cork was saturated with the tallow of many critters killed, processed and stored there.

When fire started in one of those, the Fire Department was in for a battle. Such a fire in the old Armour plant was a perfect example.

John was flying traffic that morning, but the fire didn't look like much from the air. Fire companies had been there about three hours. It didn't seem particularly big.

Nonetheless, when John landed the airplane, he drove to the fire scene. He recalls the vacant building was about a block square, brick, and seven stories tall. Its outward appearance gave little clue to what was happening inside.

Glancing around, John noticed fire trucks as close as 20 feet from the building. He talked to the battalion chief who assured him it was no big deal, and "we've got a pretty good handle on it." The next few minutes would add that remark to the list of famous last words.

John then noticed "gritty" flakes hitting his helmet and coat. He told the chief it felt like bits of mortar. This got the chief's attention quickly. As he shouted to the crews to get the aerials lowered and get the trucks and the firemen away from the building, bricks began falling. The old building was coming apart. John and the chief both saw a large crack starting at the base of the building and working its way upward. As it got to the top, it started down in a different direction, and it was clearly time to run. All the while the shower of ancient mortar and bricks increased, hitting several of the fire trucks, but somehow did not seriously hurt any of the men.

John wasn't alone at the fire scene. He recalls that Sam Feeback, the big cameraman from Channel Four, was there, as was Montie Finnell, the stocky little former Marine Master Sergeant for Channel Nine. John was in good company. All the newsmen there were quite busy now, the cameramen filming as sections of the building began to fall.

John was screaming into the two-way radio to the newsroom, "I've got to get on the air NOW!"

In an instant John was on the air live ... "Listen to this. This old building is now opening up, after burning for several hours inside. You can hear the roar and the thud as the huge walls crash to the ground. You can look in there as the walls pull apart and see each floor burning ... each an individual volcano. As the sides open up, the fire sucks air in, feeds itself and sends flame and heavy black smoke out the top. Seven floors of brick and debris just opened up like a volcano! The men are safe, but we are losing equipment; the trucks are taking a pounding from a shower of bricks! This fire is far from over!"

That's what KMBC radio listeners heard the day John recalls looking into a "living, breathing monster, making a hissing, screaming sound, like an enraged animal."

Then John caught his breath, glanced over and saw the cameramen getting great shots for their respective television stations, but can't remember any other radio men there. It's irrelevant. They weren't needed. They should have been home taking notes on John's KMBC broadcasts. On radio the story was his alone.

His coverage that day was one more example why Kansas City radio listeners were beginning to realize that when big news was breaking, their representative at the scene was John Wagner. And it certainly didn't hurt KMBC's audience ratings.

This resulted in many more "attaboys" in John's file at the station.

Competing stations were painfully aware that they could fight back only with records and golden-voiced disc jockeys. But they had to be praying that no more big news stories would break. For when the sirens sounded, other radio stations were completely at the mercy of John Wagner, and he had none for his competitors.

As the 1960s rolled on, Clarence Kelley began to put into place the law enforcement innovations that would propel the Kansas City Police Department to the head of the list of outstanding police departments in the United States. His ideas were revolutionary, and their success depended on public approval and cooperation.

Chief Kelley was a brilliant leader who knew the only way to get word to the public was through the press. He was equally brilliant in dealing with editors and reporters. One of his favorites was John Wagner.

John, by now well established as one of the best street reporters in the business, was enthusiastic about Kelley's ideas.

One was Operation One Hundred, a police tactical maneuver designed to deal with an armed person barricaded, with or without hostages, in a building or vehicle. The objective was to remove the person from the situation without harm to the officers, the public or the individual. The name of the operation was based on the fact that up to 100 officers would be involved.

John Wagner covered scores of these operations in an informative and exciting manner, often getting quite close to the action (too close for present day small-minded police commanders who think all reporters and photographers belong in pens).

It worked well. The problem incidents were handled with minimal bloodshed, most often none at all. The police looked good. The public was well served by its police and well informed by the press, especially by John Wagner.

Another Kelley idea was the Metro Squad. It was designed to help smaller police departments deal with major crime investigations that in the past had overwhelmed them.

Kelley designed the whole thing. It provided investigators

from other departments to help a jurisdiction with a big case, usually a murder. It was directed by a board of directors made up of sheriffs and chiefs of departments across the metropolitan area. When a member department needed help with a big case, the Metro Squad board of directors was called and almost immediately voted to send help.

By the time a squad could be assembled, John Wagner was already involved in covering the story. By the time the squad members arrived at the host department, if they had their car radios on, they already knew from Wagner what they would be facing. They didn't mind a bit. They enjoyed their new fame; John enjoyed covering their spectacular successes, and Chief Kelley was quite pleased with the whole thing.

The first three Metro Squad investigations were successful. The first case was broken quickly in Kansas City, Kansas. Cases two and three were more complicated and didn't break immediately.

Case two was the murder of a young Claycomo, Missouri housewife. Case three involved murders of two women from Camden Point in Platte County, Missouri. The crimes were complicated because they turned out to be the work of the same killer, who was very slick.

John began broadcasting information that the suspect car was a light-colored two-tone Buick, bearing an unusual insurance company sticker on one of the bumpers.

The search went on for several days, and then the break came. Someone in the police tow lot saw such a sticker. The only problem was that the car was not light green and white, but black. Closer examination revealed the "black Buick" was created by a few cans of cheap dime-store spray paint. The car, abandoned and unnoticed, had been in the tow lot for some time. It was the wanted car and led to the killer, who is doing life in Jefferson City.

Elza Hatfield, handpicked by Clarence Kelley to direct most of the early Metro Squad investigations, never won any prizes for being a nice guy, because he wasn't one. But he did win many honors for being a first class detective who sent far more than the normal share of bad guys to the penitentiary and some to death row.

Hatfield, a Kansas City police lieutenant when the first squad was formed, retired years later as a major. The legendary Hatfield, it was said, ate ten-penny nails for breakfast and gnawed on anyone who complicated one of his investigations. Woe be to the young detective or police officer who committed one of these sins. Hatfield elevated the 30-minute chewing out to an art form. When he was displeased, which was often, it was no secret to anyone within earshot. He yelled at reporters, too. The timid ones stayed away from him. John Wagner was not timid. He yelled back, and somehow John and the "Iron Major" became friends.

Though Hatfield yelled and threatened, John always got the information he wanted and always ended up in the right place when a big arrest was pulled off, often with Hatfield's help.

During a particularly difficult M Squad investigation based in Kansas City, Kansas police headquarters, Hatfield chased John out of the squad room. Hatfield was close behind, yelling, threatening. Wagner was running for his life. Wagner dived under a stairway while the furious Hatfield stood over him, swearing and making physical threats.

John had learned that the Kansas City, Kansas police chief had been conducting his own private investigation of the murder for political reasons and was complicating the work of the Metro Squad. When Wagner broadcast that on the radio, Hatfield went ballistic. The stairwell conversation:

Hatfield: "What the hell are you trying to do, destroy the Metro Squad?"

Wagner: "No, I'm trying to save it."

Hatfield: "Well, at the rate you're going, we'll soon be out of business."

Wagner: "Tell me one thing, Elza."

Hatfield: "What's that?"

Wagner: "Is what I said true?"

Hatfield: "Well, yes ..."

Wagner (climbing out from under the stairway and puffing out his chest): "Well, get out of my way then."

He walked right past Hatfield and out of the building. He got away with his life. Observers may not have known it, but Wagner and Hatfield really liked each other. A number of lawmen got along well with John and liked and helped him.

One was Mark Ruckel, who later retired as Chief of Detectives. Others: Jim Newman who should have succeeded Clarence Kelley as chief, but didn't. Earl "Red" Horner of Homicide, Herb McCoy of Traffic, Jim Zimmerman of Homicide, Floyd Foster of Robbery. Also Sidney Harlow, Bill Ponessa, Ron Closterman, Bob Sawtelle, Joe Pilsl, Bob Kinser, Art "Pappy" Jenkins and many others. John fears leaving off some he liked, and for that reason won't try to list them all.

There are others he didn't like. Don't look for their names in this volume.

Chapter 5

COVERING THE BIG STORIES ...

BY THE TIME these and other stories were covered, the people of Greater Kansas City had become accustomed to getting their news "live" and certainly exciting, on KMBC, all from one man.

It wasn't all cops and robbers and big fires. John became a regular "pain in the neck" to city officials as he prowled the corridors of city halls in the area. A city official once confided, "I really dreaded to see Wagner bounding into my office and shoving that microphone in my face."

John never missed an opportunity to remind his audience that one of those Kansas City, Missouri councilmen was a nephew of a top Jackson County political boss who had very close (as close as you can get) Mafia links.

In January 1965 Winston Churchill died in England. He had ties to Kansas City as a close friend of Joyce Hall, founder of Hallmark Cards. Churchill and native Kansan, Dwight Eisenhower, had planned the D-Day invasion together.

After leaving the White House in 1961, Eisenhower lived in southern California. It was from there he flew to Kansas City to pick up Joyce Hall for the longer trip to Churchill's funeral in England.

When the Air Force Jetstar rolled to a stop in Kansas City that chilly morning, several newsmen were waiting. During refueling, Eisenhower stepped from the plane and spoke with several, including John Wagner. He shared some of his memories of the wartime Prime Minister.

Ike speaking with newsmen, including the "famous crewcut" in 1965

The one Kansas City television that planned to carry Ike's visit "live" was trapped by fate. The fuel truck parked with its rear dual wheels on the television audio cable and wouldn't move. As Eisenhower conducted his "tarmac news conference" out of range of the TV station's microphone, that channel's viewers heard only the frustrated reporter's voice, but saw on camera Wagner's interview with Eisenhower. Those things happen.

Soon the plane took off for Washington, another aircraft change, and the flight to London. Behind were several newsmen, including John Wagner who enjoys remembering how he played even a very small role in a quite historic event that January day alongside a Kansas City airport runway.

On a day John will not soon forget he had to say good-bye to the big black Mercury sedan that had served him well from his KMBC beginnings as Unit Thirteen. It's always tough to say farewell to a faithful friend when you've "totalled" that friend in a wreck. The replacement was a white Mustang which became Wagner's new office ... by executive order.

John had caught General Manager Dave Croninger's attention by spending too much time in the office, advising other station employees on how they should be doing their work, and sharing his dislike for sports, and for the people who report sports.

Croninger solved the problem by informing John: "You were hired to work on the street. From now on I never want to see you in the office again except on payday, and at the Christmas party." John took the not-so-subtle hint and went to the streets and even had some notepads made to prove it. The white Mustang became the Wagner office.

At about that time KMBC added a dimension to its already dazzling news operation. The station leased a helicopter and hired one of the Police Department's trained pilots. Corporal Tom Prudden usually flew it, and Sgt. Frank Kohler rode as observer and broadcast traffic reporter known as the KMBC Trafficopter.

Unit Thirteen was making its round one spring morning

THIS IS THE OFFICE OF
JOHN WAGNER

_____

_____

_____

_____

_____

_____

_____

_____

_____

_____

When the boss says keep out of the office, you move outside.
Wagner did.

when John intercepted a police call, advising cars that a woman had just jumped into the Kaw River from the James Street bridge in Kansas City, Kansas. Survival is rare in those cases.

John, assuming he would be searching for a dead body, moved toward the confluence of the Kaw and Missouri Rivers at the foot of Municipal Airport.

By now the helicopter was overhead, sweeping both the rivers in an effort to find some trace of the woman. Suddenly Prudden and Kohler saw the woman clinging to a brush-covered sandbar three miles from where she jumped. Wagner hurried to a spot nearby.

By radio John urged Prudden to land the copter at water's edge to rescue the woman. Prudden, careful and wise pilot, decided it was too risky and elected to go farther ashore, land on firmer terrain, and allow John to scramble aboard, taking Kohler's seat.

The helicopter went back up and out over the little sandbar, dipped to about 25 feet off the water, and circled. John handed Prudden the newsreel camera he always carried for KMBC's sister station (Channel 9), grabbed the marked KMBC blanket and his walkie talkie, and jumped out, landing in water right beside the little island.

There he found 67-year-old Sue Hass, somewhat dazed but otherwise all right. Always the broadcast reporter, John went on the air immediately, interviewed the lady, assured her family she had lived through the ordeal, and swore to spank her if she ever tried anything like that again.

John said: "Susie, you don't have a worry in the world. Do you know you just took a three-mile swim and survived?"

The interview and John's daring jump into the river from the helicopter filled the air that morning. As Wagner broadcast from the sandbar, Prudden circled overhead filming the incident for television.

Other news outfits began to gather at the opposite bank of the river, helpless to intrude on John Wagner's dramatic story. All they could do was watch as a Corps of Engineers boat moved toward the little dot where Wagner and Mrs. Hass were waiting for rescue.

Only the *Kansas City Star* could do anything about it. That evening's front page showed Wagner's picture with his arm and a KMBC blanket around the woman as they walked ashore from the boat. The caption ignored Wagner, referring to him only as an unknown observer. The paper and others could not bring themselves to admit that they had been beaten, badly, by an upstart radio reporter, but they were.

While the incident was one of the most dramatic of John Wagner's career, it was continuing proof of the energy and inventiveness he brought to the job. John was following a pattern he had established earlier in his life. He was truly cocky, pushy and at times smart aleck ... necessary characteristics for a good street reporter. He was in a class all by himself.

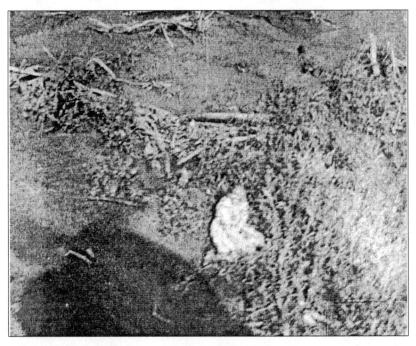

67-year-old Sue Hass shown on the sand bar in the Missouri Rover. This is how she looked to Corporal Tom Prudden as he first discovered her.

John Wagner is shown with the woman on the sand bar, and a Corps of Engineers boat is shown about to rescue them both. Even as this picture was taken, John was giving an on-air report.

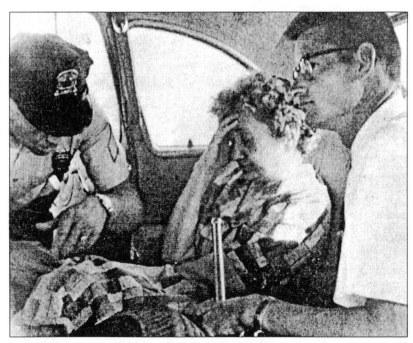

Safely back to shore, Mrs. Hass is shown sitting with KMBC newsman John Wagner as they await an ambulance. A somewhat happy ending to what could have been a serious situation.

The management of the radio station realized what it had in Wagner. Ratings were high. Business was good, and if anyone wanted to know what was happening on the streets, while it was happening, KMBC was the place to be.

Walt Lochman, manager of the station in later years, said long after he retired that John Wagner had revolutionized the business of news reporting on radio in Kansas City. Not only that. He redefined it and demonstrated how radio could be used for dramatic news coverage.

Lochman was manager for the new owner of the radio station, Bonneville Broadcasting, which bought the radio station from Metromedia and changed the call letters to KMBZ.

John's car was displaying those new call letters one spring day when he was "cruising," going nowhere in particular, but just trying to put himself in the part of town where things usually happened. It could have been Linwood, Armour, Paseo, Prospect, Troost. This time it happened to be Independence Avenue.

That was a good choice. John was only blocks away when the police radio reported the armed robbery of a savings and loan office near Independence and Prospect.

The Mustang got there right behind a police car driven by Officer Bill Pruitt. John broadcast his arrival at the bank and noticed that a very excited man was waving at the police car and got in. Pruitt assumed the man was one of the robbery victims.

John followed as the police car raced away to the east. It came to a park where John saw another man holding another police officer at gunpoint against a tree.

Wagner broadcast the entire event as Pruitt pulled the police car onto the grass and got out with his shotgun. Pruitt quickly realized that his "passenger" was not a victim, but was one of the bad guys and was holding a gun.

The quick-thinking young policeman used to practice off-duty with a shotgun by throwing rocks into the air and blasting them before they could hit the ground. This day he wasn't shooting at rocks. He was taking two dangerous men off the

John and his famous and well-travelled Unit 13

street. Two quick blasts from the police riot gun accomplished that. Case closed. Call the coroner.

It had to be a scary moment for Officer Pruitt when he realized that he had picked up one of the bandits left behind at the bank, and that the man could have killed him anytime while he was riding in the police car.

The officer being held at gunpoint had stopped the getaway car, was disarmed and overpowered by the first robber. Pruitt's quick action saved the lives of two policemen.

And John Wagner's audience heard the entire story as it happened from his dangerous vantage point: the middle of the gun battle.

Years later the story was recreated by a national television show that features big crime stories. Right in the middle of the original news film, used as a basis for the show, stood John Wagner with his crewcut and the White Mustang.

Despite their bad luck, hoodlums till can't resist the temptation to rob banks in the Kansas City area. They usually end up in prison or the morgue, but they keep trying.

The Metcalf State Bank at Metcalf Avenue and Santa Fe Drive in Overland Park, Kansas was picked as a target by second-rate ex-convicts, Henry Floyd Brown and Andrew Evan Gipson. Working with a pair of women companions, Brown and Gipson thought they had it figured.

In January of 1968 the women applied theatrical makeup to the two thugs. They dyed Brown's hair dark brown and bleached Gipson's hair nearly white.

The plan: Set off a bomb on the steps of Overland Park City Hall as a diversion and rob the bank. All the while the two bank robbers were in walkie talkie contact with their women, who were watching the whole thing from a pancake restaurant across Metcalf.

Fleeing the bank, they fired a machine gun at a pursuing Overland Park policeman. Lucky fellow was nicked in the lip.

All this excitement quickly came to John Wagner's attention, but he was inside Kansas City, Missouri's City Hall miles away. While he was violating the speed limit heading toward Overland Park, John heard a description of the getaway car. He quickly radioed KMBZ and put that information on the air. He urged people to look out their windows, and if they see such a car, call his radio station or the police.

Meanwhile, Overland Park Police, under Chief John Kenyan, were trying to react to the big crime. FBI agents, headed by Assistant Special Agent in Charge of the Kansas City office, Charles "Buck" Henry, were steaming toward the bank.

Henry and Agent Jim Cassidy were in the bank when word came that a likely getaway car had been spotted at an apartment complex ... thanks to John Wagner's appeal for public help. A citizen heard John's appeal, looked out a window of the Heatherwood Apartments at 85th and Robinson about a mile from the bank, and called KMBZ with the information. News Director Max Bicknell took the call and quickly informed the FBI.

By this time John Wagner was getting into Overland Park and headed right for the apartment complex, where a brief shooting war was about to break out. John remembers arriving just behind a Kansas Highway Patrol car. As the two cars approached the building, Wagner heard a gunshot. He stopped and backed up. The patrol car stopped and reversed, then turned onto a curved driveway in front of the apartment building with the white Mustang right behind.

Just then another shot was fired from the building, and John could no longer see the trooper. Wagner was outside the car by now and crouched between the news car and the patrol car.

The second shot hit Patrol Sgt. Eldon Miller in the head and hurled him into the back seat. He was DOA at a hospital.

All the while John, only a few feet from the dying policeman, was broadcasting what was happening ... and much of it, including the gunshots, could be heard by his listeners.

An army of lawmen quickly gathered. FBI Agent Walt Witchard headed a special entry team to go into the building. FBI Agent Joe Kissiah handled the tear gas gun. FBI Agent Tony Lehman and countless other G-men were outside in a firing position. Captain Myron Scafe headed Overland Park Police efforts to get into the building.

Just then a bomb, an explosive-packed soft drink can wrapped in tape, was rolled out on the lawn at the police. The snow put out the sputtering fuse.

After more volleys of gunfire and some more tear gas, the agents and police went inside. Of course, Wagner went with them.

They found only Brown, wounded but still alive. He and Gipson had split, each taking half the bank loot. The women were nowhere around. They and Gipson were arrested later.

When it was over, everyone there had to stop and catch a breath. Many were feeling the effects of the tear gas. Most of the lawmen had never been in a shootout like that one, and few would ever be again.

There were few, if any, winners that day. The Kansas Highway Patrol had lost its first officer in the line of duty. Sadly, Sgt. Eldon Miller was not the last Kansas trooper to be killed. The bank got its money back. Prison gates opened wide for Brown, Gipson and the two women.

Thirty years later Brown was out of prison and was quoted as saying he wanted to get married, have children and own a house. Sgt. Eldon Miller would like a normal life, too. His was cut short by bank robber and cop killer Henry Floyd Brown.

In retrospect, if there were any winners that day, they were probably the radio listeners who followed the crime and the gun battle on John Wagner's broadcasts. They were truly spectacular. And he could feel some sense of accomplishment, too. For if he had not broadcast the appeal for the getaway car, the four people involved might have pulled off the perfect crime.

It was another Wagner demonstration of a new dimension in coverage of live news by radio.

Chapter 6

RIOTS IN KANSAS CITY

A FEW MONTHS LATER, in April of 1968, Rev. Martin Luther King, Jr. was shot to death at a Memphis, Tennessee motel. The murder was committed on Friday evening, April 4th.

There was immediate street mob reaction in Detroit, Washington, D.C., and in New York, complete with shooting, looting and burning.

Similar groups in Kansas City were not too nice to break the law. They just weren't that well organized yet. The weekend that followed the killing was tense; little happened, but it was merely a matter of time.

Monday it started. An assembly, planned as a memorial service to King, was scheduled at Central High School, a mostly black school at Linwood and Indiana, several miles southeast of downtown.

Otis Taylor and Curtis McClinton, Kansas City Chiefs football players, who happened to be black men, were there. McClinton, whose singing talents matched his football abilities, was performing.

But the memorial service assembly was not what the teenagers wanted. They wanted out of there. They wanted to march somewhere and do something, perhaps raise some hell.

Newsman Wagner was reporting traffic from the air that morning and noted that some small groups were running through downtown, knocking down elderly women shoppers and breaking a few windows.

One has to be careful about reporting such incidents in tense times. No one wanted to drop the match in the powder.

He landed at the airport and drove to his east-side home, a daily custom. On normal days he would take time to have coffee and some breakfast. This would not be a normal day.

The news director was on the phone, informing John that things were getting out of hand on the streets. Near rioting, if not the real thing, was underway in several places.

What's more, a huge crowd was moving out of Central High and headed downtown. That, of course, was the last thing the Kansas City Police Department commanders wanted.

Under the brilliant leadership of Chief Clarence Kelley, police were out in force. Missouri Governor Warren Hearnes was notified. The governor ordered the Missouri State Highway Patrol and Missouri National Guard to get troops moving toward Kansas City.

The state-controlled Kansas City Police Department is supervised by a board of commissioners, appointed by the governor of Missouri. The mayor of Kansas City is an ex-officio member, by virtue of his elected office.

Mayor Ilus Davis was quickly notified and briefed by Chief Kelley. The mayor immediately left City Hall in a car driven by a police officer and went out to meet the crowd from Central High, the mayor's old school.

At several points along the way the hundreds of teenagers were met by long lines of police officers, who would let them pass at the last minute. The mood was ugly. Ministers walking along with them warned newsmen along the way to be careful. It was dangerous. No one has yet explained why breaking windows and throwing rocks are considered natural expressions of grief and respect.

The crowd of hundreds was met next by a police line at 18th and Paseo, not far from downtown. The mayor had now caught up with them and addressed them over a police car's loudspeaker, while standing on the hood of the car.

When he sensed he could not persuade them to stop here and go back home, he asked them where they wanted to go.

They shouted, "City Hall." He said, "I'll go with you." This was not what the police wanted to hear.

John Wagner, reporting all this on the air, was horrified when the procession, led by Mayor Davis, walked right out onto the Southeast Freeway (now I-70). He took to the air again and warned drivers their freeway was filled with pedestrians. He regarded traffic as his personal property, and anyone who complicated "his" traffic should get no favorable consideration.

The crowd filled the south lawn of City Hall. A microphone was brought out, and the mayor began speaking. No one was listening. Suddenly a bottle was thrown out of the crowd. It shattered on a walkway. Next came a teargas cannister. This was promptly answered by police who applied teargas in generous quantity. The crowd, now a furious mob, retreated east along 12th Street, breaking every pane of glass along its path. The riot was on.

John Wagner swears that the first teargas, which came out of the crowd, was actually stolen from the mayor's car while he was speaking at 18th and Paseo. A police walkie talkie was also taken from the car and was used later to try to confuse and jam police radio frequencies as officers struggled to deal with the dangerous situation. Eventually its battery ran down. City Hall sits at 12th and Oak in a civic plaza arrangement. South across 12th is the Jackson County Courthouse. East across Locust is the Police Headquarters building. The teargas made it impossible to conduct proceedings in the courthouse. All had to be delayed. The Jackson County sheriff ordered heavy security on the courthouse.

Police tightened security on their headquarters which was now the command post for the riot response. It was also impossible to enter City Hall.

But with his many contacts, Wagner could go about wherever he pleased, and did so.

The rest of Monday was reasonably quiet during the remaining daylight. At sundown a curfew went into effect.

Wagner reported frequently from many different parts of the city, noting that the extra security forces were on hand.

Newsman Wagner in the middle of the 1968 riot action surrounded by Kansas City Police

The Missouri State Highway Patrol had downtown. National Guard units, many of them heavily armed Military Police, controlled everything east of downtown and north. The rest of Kansas City was protected by Kansas City Police. National Guardsmen rode on all fire trucks, and in most city police cars … two guardsmen … two policemen … gun barrels aimed out the windows. John was busy covering all the action.

Some National Guard troops were stationed in the downtown business district, on the Country Club Plaza and at Ward Parkway shopping center, lest anyone be tempted by "instant credit."

Kansas National Guard troops took up positions along the state line to ensure that any trouble that started in Kansas City, Missouri stayed there.

When the sun went down that evening, the looters came out to play. Chief Kelley had already ordered that looters would be shot. Several were delivered to emergency rooms that night for treatment of shotgun wounds ... painful pellet penetration of posterior areas. The wounds, while painful, were not fatal. It quickly removed the fun from looting.

The curfew was being tightly enforced, and scores went to jail that night. There was no long wait for arraignment. Jackson County magistrates set up court in the ground floor garage of Police Headquarters and sent the offenders to jail.

John had had a long and exciting first day of the Kansas City riots. It had been exciting, too, for KMBC listeners who had heard John reporting from, it must have seemed, all over town. He was their only instant link to the action, which they could not see first hand because of the curfew. Television couldn't do much for lack of live transmission capability, and any film shot had to be processed, taking hours. Newspapers came out the next day. For its time, for instant coverage, it was a radio story ... a John Wagner radio story.

As that first day ended, John was tired, but the excitement of it wouldn't let him stop or rest. No one knew it that first night, but the biggest, most frightening day of the riot story was just hours away.

Tuesday dawned a sunny, slightly hazy day. The haze came from lingering teargas, and the smoke from only partially extinguished fires.

Early that day it was time for social workers, preachers and the usual groups of apologists for criminal behavior to stage protests and make demands.

Some of their demands:

1. Get the police out of certain areas ... let rioters control some of the city.
2. Quit using teargas.
3. Make Chief Kelley apologize to the rioters for using gas and force.
4. Delay the imposition of the curfew Tuesday night.

Kelley responded:

1. As long as I am Chief of Police of this city, the criminal element will not control a square foot of it.

2. We will use whatever means necessary, including teargas, to maintain public safety in this city.
3. Forget any apology from me.
4. No delay in tonight's curfew. (Kelley was overruled on this one … it was delayed a few hours.)

Monday had been looting day. Tuesday would be firebombing and shooting day. With the curfew delayed several hours to keep from hurting anyone's feelings, the stage was set for a bad night.

It was not long in coming. Newsman Wagner felt the city was at war. It had all the signs … National Guardsmen riding all fire trucks, in most police cars, ambulances operated by the Fire Department had blacked-out windows and would enter a troubled area, even in an emergency, only under heavy escort.

The combined command post was set up on grounds of the World War Two Memorial building at Linwood and Paseo. John was a frequent visitor to the "CP." It came under sniper fire several times. His listeners could hear the shots.

Law-abiding black people, and Kansas City has many, suffered some embarrassing and frightening moments.

One woman, stopped for a curfew violation, told police she was taking lunch to her husband who was working at Linwood and Paseo. "A likely story, lady," said one policeman. Then someone checked. Her husband just happened to be a lieutenant colonel, second in command of National Guard troops at the command post. She got through.

A black man, Ed Wilson, a battalion fire chief, was warned by a mob that he would be killed because he was cooperating with lawful authority. When the mob moved toward him, he put the Fire Department car into reverse and drove a block and a half as fast as a Ford will go backwards. Wilson survived and lived to become, years later, chief and director of the Kansas City Fire Department.

When the sun began to sink that Tuesday evening, John Wagner could smell the electricity in the air. Little crowds were on street corners, there were shouts, raised fists, car horns were honking. He mentioned this to his listeners several times an hour.

He stopped when he saw his friend and neighbor, Police Lt. Bill Ponessa, at 31st and Prospect. Ponessa and Wagner hardly had time to exchange greetings when the officer's radio crackled with the news that a National Guardsman had been shot while riding a fire truck to a firebombing at 30th and Prospect, a short block away.

Seconds later, Wagner, Ponessa and an army of police officers were there in the first major shooting engagement of the Kansas City riots. The shot that hit the guardsman came from the three-story Byron Hotel, near the northeast corner.

Ponessa quickly decided that, before any major action could be taken, the one remaining street light at 30th and Prospect would have to be darkened. It gave the snipers firing from the Byron a big advantage.

Along with the gunfire going in both directions, Ponessa's order to shoot out the street light caused some more noise, not immediately effective. Few officers won any marksmanship ribbons for the street light effort. Finally one shot found the mark, and the light hit the pavement in pieces.

KMBC radio listeners, confined to their homes by the curfew, were at the scene by radio. They heard the gunfire and Wagner's descriptions.

To raise the price of doing battle with the police, it was decided to give the Byron Hotel some teargas. That usually takes the fight out of people. Ponessa's men began to lob gas cannisters into the building. One hit a window ledge and bounced back to the street, spewing the painful fumes into Lt. Ponessa's face. John was standing next to him and caught a mouthful, too. He helped drag Ponessa to the corner where a National Guardsman's canteen provided some welcome relief.

At that point Wagner devoted his next live report to informing the lieutenant's wife that he was okay. "Mrs. Ponessa, your husband has just taken a hit with teargas. He's hurting, but he's going to be okay. Don't worry."

Back at the front of the Byron, Ponessa and Wagner, now recovered, saw an elderly woman crouched in the front of the building. They quickly got her away from there, half leading and half dragging her.

The gunfire was heavy until police got close enough to enter the building. A loudspeaker barked, "Hold your fire … officers are in the building." When the shooting stopped, it was evident that five people had been killed … all civilians.

One other man was shot to death several blocks south of the big gun battle. He had a long police arrest and prison record, which ended with the notation, "He died while trying to ram his car through a police roadblock."

Wagner's listeners also heard that happen. He and his portable radio were nearly everywhere.

The shooting had died down to sporadic incidents in other parts of the city that Tuesday night. Fires continued to burn through the night as snipers kept firemen back. One fireman, nicked by a sniper's bullet, was young Harold Knabe who, years later, became very well known and liked throughout the area as the Fire Department's information officer.

The events of that night, the shootings, the arson fires and the other skirmishes marked the turning point of the riots. It was obvious that lawful authority was in charge and that force would be met by superior force. A few more curfew violators would be arrested and jailed, and a few more minor incidents would occur, but the major action was finished. John Wagner's reports reflected that. The city heaved a sigh of relief.

The riots were probably the biggest running story Wagner covered for KMBZ. Of course, the rescue of the lady in the river and the Metcalf Bank robbery and gun battle were big. But the riots made the biggest headlines. And John had been deeply involved in all of them.

No one who heard his descriptions and the actual sounds of battle will ever forget. He went so far as to let his listeners hear the actual sounds of walking on riot-shattered glass that covered parts of Prospect Avenue.

There would be months of hearings and investigations as

order was restored and Kansas City got its life back to normal, whatever normal is.

John Wagner, who saw and covered so much, was never asked to testify at any of the hearings. He believes he could have given investigators some valuable information.

After so many large and dramatic events, a long period of quiet settled in. Wagner's radio news work returned to a steadier, calmer, far less violent pace.

Chapter 7

TROUBLE AT THE RADIO STATION

IT WASN'T LONG before Wagner began to worry. Nothing outside the job bothered him. He wasn't afraid of competition. He was getting along well with police and firemen. Even public officials had learned to accept his way of doing things. He was beginning to feel uneasy about his job.

In the broadcasting business one has to know that a career can end in an instant, sometimes for no reason. You know it can happen, but you must never honor it by fearing it. John never really feared anything, but still something was happening.

One day he was called in to the front office and was told that one of his recent reports had generated complaints from listeners. The story concerned an armed robbery of the workmen repairing a crime-infested public housing project at the east side of downtown. John had referred to the criminal as "a young punk with a gun." The manager insisted John had called him a "young BLACK punk with a gun."

John denied all, and no action against him was taken. Still John regarded this as another sign of trouble. You don't spend the years Wagner had spent on the streets and fail to notice gathering storm clouds.

"I knew trouble was coming. I could smell it in the air."

The feeling wasn't helped when the manager, Walt Lochman, called John into the office to meet someone ... a new news director. Lochman had just fired the other one.

"I went in there and saw this guy sitting there, overweight, slouched down like he owned the place, instead of sitting like a man should."

He recalls learning later that the new news director was a buddy of one of the disc jockeys (who was a certified drunk), and what's more was a drinking buddy of the station executive. Not a good sign.

Another worse sign, from Wagner's perspective, came a few days later when the new man said he had heard much about John and wanted to ride with him for a while.

John says, "The guy got into the car, and as I started the engine, all my police and fire radios came on, 40 of them. He asked, "How do you turn this garbage off? I want to talk."

John replied, "Are you crazy? A guy still working here nearly got fired for turning down the radios in the newsroom."

New news director: "I don't care. I can't talk with those things on."

Wagner thought: "Uh, oh, this is the end."

It wasn't the immediate end, but later events supported all of John's early suspicions.

The actual end came later when Lochman called John in again and told him things were changing and many things are going on. He handed Wagner a beautifully written letter of recommendation. "This letter concerns the abilities of mobile news reporter John Wagner ... etc."

Beautiful words notwithstanding, dated September 3, 1969, it still meant that after six years, during which he had played a major role in lifting the station to the top of the audience ratings and risked his neck many times, KMBC had fallen out of love with the guy who helped put it where it was. He was fired.

Badly beaten down, his pride in ruins, Wagner thought of the 12 years he had spent in broadcasting. Most of the days had been good, but not always without problems. "As I looked back, I realized that most of my problems had come from people who spent their lives sitting behind desks — salesmen, program directors — all of them former disc jockeys — and others who never got out on the street, never got dirty or too hot or too cold, or were never shot at. These are the people who got very nervous when I would describe a news situation a little too colorfully. Because of that, and because of them, I decided to get out of the business."

That's easier said than done. Though he had covered virtually every kind of crime and calamity, John was not prepared to enter the "business" world.

Chapter 8

WAGNER AND THE CHAIR

JOHN'S BACKGROUND and inner passion cost him one job opportunity. He submitted to a pre-employment polygraph, lie detector, test by a prospective employer. During the test an ambulance went by with siren blaring. The dolt administering the test flunked him. After all, who wants to hire anyone who reacts to a siren? Better yet, who ever expected John Wagner NOT to react to a siren?

A few days later Wagner found employment, briefly, with an employment agency, which takes money from the unemployed to help them find employment. He spent a week there, then left, saying his conscience would not allow him to go on. He called it "white slavery."

Then, without a job or a paycheck, John remembered he had always had a friendly relationship with Bob Goodfriend, one of the big guns of the Durwood theater chain. Durwood owned the Capri Theater in the same building housing KMBZ. It took only one phone call.

John's first assignment for Durwood, ironically, was to manage the Capri. "Guess who worked downstairs? Walt Lochman, the guy who fired me."

It was about the time that KMBZ's owners had completed construction of a new building in Westwood, Kansas. The station was moving out of its long-time downtown Kansas City home.

The moving process, historically, has been complicated by

the fact that broadcasters are generally pack rats. Nonetheless, the movers organized the heavy part of the job fairly well. Big equipment and furniture were moved up to lobby level from the below-street-level radio station and held in an open lobby just outside the theater manager's office. Then trucks came by on the Central Avenue side, and crews loaded the items.

Wagner, now boss of the Capri, recognized among the furnishings a handsome black leather executive chair waiting to be picked up. It was a dandy, sat on a swivel, had a high "big boss" back, nice wide padded leather arms and was Walt Lochman's pride and joy. The next truck wouldn't be there for at least half an hour. No one was watching. Temptation conquered all. Walt Lochman's prize chair rolled past the curtained archway separating broadcast station from theater, and it came to a stop in the theater manager's office. Later on a dark, quiet night it was moved to Wagner's home in east Kansas City, never again to support the posterior of a radio station manager.

John recalls: "I figured I owed Walt a good one. Besides, the statute of limitations ran out years ago. The last laugh was mine."

The movers and radio station employees, at Lochman's command, beat the place apart trying to find Walt's chair. They never did.

Chapter 9

MOVING ON TO WDAF

JOHN WAS GETTING ALONG with his career in the Durwood Theater group. He learned quickly about profit and loss columns and was able to use some of the discipline he encountered at the hands of the nuns back at St. Henry's school in Chicago so many years earlier.

When there was a problem, I was sent in to fix it. Theft by employees was a big problem. So was cleanliness. I straightened out some ushers who came to work looking like bums. And after some unpleasantness, my staff came to work with clean white shirts, pressed pants, shined shoes and no hair showing below the ears."

He recalls some people were stealing from the concession stand. He caught a janitor selling company-owned supplies. Those problems were wiped out quickly.

"I cleaned up a theft problem at Indian Springs. I cleaned up theft and vandalism at the Metro Theater complex. Then one day I was called in and introduced to a man they wanted me to train as a manager. I later learned he was to be a district manager. He wanted me to help him entrap and fire other managers ... a hatchet man. I looked him in the eye and said, "I won't fink for you. Do your own dirty work. My job ended right there."

So four and a half years after being bounced at KMBZ, John found himself on the streets again without a job or a paycheck. But before despair could get too deep, "One day I got a call from my old friend, Charles Gray. He wanted me to join him at WDAF, to fly the airplane and cover traffic and handle some ground news coverage."

John's first assignment was to go directly to the airport and pick up the airplane. He was on his way, mentally reviewing flight procedures, memorizing the broadcast schedule, rehearsing how to do the job.

Suddenly his old yellow pickup truck broke down on a busy interstate highway. His first thought: "Oh, no, I can't miss my first assignment for WDAF!" He managed to nudge the truck to the side of the road, got out and ran half a mile to a pay phone to report his predicament to Gray.

"Not to worry ... Dan Henry will come out and pick you up."

John says: "That's when I got to meet Dan Henry, one of a kind, one in a million." (Everyone who ever knew Dan Henry agrees with that assessment.)

"Thanks to Dan Henry, I got to the airport and did my first traffic (and my first flying) in nearly five years. By golly, it worked."

Chapter 9

WAGNER BEGINS WDAF CAREER

AFTER SURVIVING the breakdown of his truck on his first day at WDAF, John went right to work cementing old relationships with his major news contacts.

The Kansas City Police Department was making final preparations for its observance of Memorial Day, a service that honors fallen policemen. John always attended.

He was at Police Headquarters at 12th and Locust downtown where he was quickly reacquainted with Clarence Kelley, former police chief, and then director of the FBI. Kelley was accompanied by Dr. Joseph D. McNamara, his immediate successor as police chief.

John chatted briefly with both men, noting that the famous police monument had been moved to headquarters from its original space at 59th and Paseo.

John glanced diagonally across the street to the Jackson County Courthouse where a window washer was working high up on the 13-story building.

As John watched, the rope holding the small platform for the window washer slipped or broke, dropping the poor fellow many feet to about the third floor, where he was dangling by just one thin rope just outside a courtroom. The terrified man interrupted a trial. It's hard to concentrate on evidence when a man is hanging just outside the window and screaming for his life.

John raced across the street and began broadcasting a

rapid-fire report on the man's predicament, even before Fire Department rescue teams got there. It was dramatic coverage and good to hear once again, since Kansas City radio had become so dull in John's long absence.

Fortunately, the terrified window washer was brought down safely, and the story ended well. But it put John Wagner back into action in dramatic fashion.

The next day a downtown bank was robbed by criminals who fled to the old north end, the public housing projects at 5th and Harrison, a neighborhood swarming with narcotics and narcotics criminals.

John went with the police into the projects and covered the sounds of the arrest live on WDAF. It was as though he had never been away.

WDAF was in for some exciting days that would last until terminal disc jockey mentality would find some way to destroy him.

Chapter 10

THE McNAMARA DAYS

JOSEPH McNAMARA, holder of a Doctorate in Public Administration (sometimes erroneously called a Ph.D by his zealous backers), took over the Kansas City Police Department leadership not long after John Wagner became WDAF's one-man SWAT team.

The two were bound to collide. McNamara was a hardheaded Irishman from the New York City Police Department, and Wagner's German skull was about the same grade of granite.

Complicating the whole picture was the fact that very few of the Kansas City officers had any use for McNamara. And Wagner, newsman that he was, picked that up very quickly.

To be completely fair, McNamara, or even God himself, would have had trouble stepping into the big shoes of Clarence Kelley, who left Kansas City to be FBI director. It was simply too big an act to follow.

McNamara, fresh from the Knapp Commission days on NYPD, was convinced there was corruption on KCPD. And sure enough, he found it when several of his Kansas City cops turned up dirty in a theft ring targeting a large warehouse near the Missouri River. The culprits were fired and prosecuted.

John Wagner proved completely loyal to the source who kept him posted on all details of the investigation from the very beginning. High-ranking police officers and even the FBI were baffled as to how the big secret was penetrated. Chief McNamara later admitted that John Wagner and this writer knew more about KCPD than he did.

A deal is a deal ... and no word of the case was leaked until one Sunday morning when the offenders were arrested and the story broke on WDAF, thanks to John Wagner.

To this day Wagner has not confided the name of the source who led him to one of the most embarrassing and shameful news stories in the history of the Kansas City Police Department.

All the while, McNamara's relationship with the officers on his force continued to deteriorate. One captain, Robert Heinen, was a thorn in McNamara's side, which enhanced Heinen's standing with many other members of the department.

Painted signs reading "Viva Heinen" appeared on public buildings, including a police station, and on railroad over-passes. The paint was very high quality. The words were still legible 25 years later.

The public not only saw the signs, but heard them mentioned on the radio when John used them as landmarks in news stories or traffic reports, i.e., "Traffic is really messed up beginning about 100 feet east of the Heinen railroad bridge." And somehow, everyone who heard knew what and where he meant.

John's aggressiveness and uncanny ability to be in the right place at the right time continued to develop. One evening while awaiting the arrival of President Gerald Ford at Municipal Airport, a smiling Chief McNamara asked a WDAF newsman: "Which way is John Wagner going to come at us tonight?"

Among most of the traffic policemen, John was a favorite. His WDAF News car was frequently the last one in a presidential motorcade, having been waved into position as the police motorcycles closed the end of the procession around him. He was known as Tail End Charlie.

He used that good relationship to great effect during the

1976 Republican National Convention in Kansas City. He was on a borrowed motorcycle, bearing a handmade license plate 610 ... the frequency of WDAF. His mission was to cover the demonstrations plus the arrivals and departures of VIP motorcades.

The motorcade coverage was no problem. But when a group of homosexuals began a noisy demonstration for God knows what, in the assigned demonstration area, John was covering their antics live on WDAF and briefly forgot an inoffensive way to describe such creatures. Wisely discarding the usual station-house descriptions, he came up with "switch hitters." It was truly colorful, interesting and descriptive radio.

Other stations in the Taft Broadcasting chain sent reporters and executives to Kansas City for the convention. The manager of the company's Columbus, Ohio station was trying to get to Kemper Arena for his credentials. He couldn't get through the tight security. He hadn't checked into his hotel and still had his luggage when he spotted the Wagner motorcycle with the 610 license plate. Somehow he managed to get Wagner's attention and told his story. Wagner, always the doubting cop at heart, didn't believe him, but radioed the company headquarters at the arena to check him out.

When the man proved he was who he said he was, Wagner was very helpful. He hailed a police car and asked the officers to take the man to the front door of the arena, past security, where his credentials would be waiting. That's how Jim Pidcock, manager of the Taft station WTVN in Columbus, Ohio, got to the Republican convention. He was impressed by John Wagner and was even more impressed an hour later when the police called to ask where they could deliver Mr. Pidcock's luggage.

That was just one of WDAF's memories of the GOP convention. The station broadcast the entire convention, gavel to gavel.

Engineer Wes Wheeler re-wired the station's standard two-way radio system to feed to a broadcast line out of Kemper Arena. Otherwise walkie talkie signals could not penetrate the walls of Kemper Arena. The station had only three walkie talkies. One was carried by Wagner on the motorcycle. One was shared on the convention floor by WDAF reporters Caroline Rooney and Larry Kanter, who had to hand it back and forth. And the third was in the broadcast booth, where it was used to communicate with the floor and the motorcycle.

It was a high point in station history, but could never happen again because it would take too much time away from disc jockeys.

Three television networks, two radio networks, all carrying the convention, plus a local UHF TV station and a local radio station carrying the Royals in a pennant race were WDAF's competition for listeners that week.

Still, it had to be done, and John Wagner had a hand in it.

Chapter 11

WAGNER HITS THE STREETS

QUITE EARLY in John's WDAF career he had some catching up to do. He had been away from his regular haunts for several years. Many of his old contacts had retired or transferred, and a number of newer people had come to the police and fire departments. They were strangers to him, and they certainly did not know him.

That was made quite clear one morning in his early WDAF days when he intercepted a police radio call describing a gang rape in progress in an apartment building in a shady part of midtown Kansas City.

He was wearing a business suit, and no signs declaring he was a newsman. He bounded up the stairway with a young uniformed policeman and reached the second floor apartment where the "crime" was underway.

The policeman kicked the door open, then turned to John and said, "I've got about a dozen in here."

John replied with much bravado, "Send them out here in the hall and I'll stack them against the wall."

John got his bluff in early on the suspects (which means they feared for their lives). Other officers got there quickly and determined it was not rape but an assignation; that is, the young woman consented to her situation.

And it ended. The two, Wagner and the young policeman, went back to their respective cars, Wagner to prepare a broadcast report, the policeman to fill out his report forms.

Still believing John was a plain clothes detective, the officer asked Wagner for his badge number. When told John had no badge and was a WDAF newsman, the blood drained from the policeman's face. He had just placed his life in the hands of a reporter. Older officers assured the young man he was in good hands. They believed, for good reason, if you have to trust your fate to one newsman, John Wagner is the best choice.

That officer retired in the mid-1990s, but still remembers the day.

Soon John Wagner's relationship with the policeman on the street was as strong as ever, perhaps stronger. Stronger because he was so much more visible. He was covering traffic from the air in morning and afternoon rush hours and in between was covering fast-breaking, exciting news on the street.

This gave him double contact with police. They have to handle traffic, and they have to deal with crime. And in those days they also dealt with John, for it seemed he was everywhere. He paid particular attention to the parts of town where action was most likely.

One street was Truman Road, also known as 15th Street. It runs east and west from downtown Kansas City out east through Independence. And it provides handy access to major north-south streets in eastern Kansas City.

All those elements made Central Bank at 3030 Truman Road a tempting target for bank robbers. It was "hit" many times.

By now Sylvester Young, Junior, the bad son of a good policeman was out of the penitentiary. Young Syl had been sent away after being caught in that downtown jewelry company holdup, where John Wagner and Clarence Kelley crossed paths for the first time.

Old habits, being hard to break, sent Syl to Central Bank with a gun in his hand and robbery on his mind. His escape was nearly blocked by traffic officer Bill Hudson. But Hudson's pursuit ended when Young fired several shots into the police car radiator.

All the while John Wagner was broadcasting the robbery

story, details of the brief shootout and a description of the getaway car on WDAF.

John's instincts sent him to a neighborhood where he was certain Young was heading. When he saw the escape car sitting in a driveway, he thought he was right. When a shot was fired at the WDAF News car, he knew he was right.

Thinking quickly, John decided to run with police into a house next door to where Young was holed up.

The block was sealed off, and John was trapped with a group of policemen, without cigarettes, in a house next door to a trigger-happy bank robber.

Wagner made the most of his situation. WDAF was broadcasting live from the center of a breaking story, while competitors were held at barricades a block away.

It was Wagner at his best. He even described smoke pouring from the back of the house. The bank robber was burning thousands of dollars on the kitchen stove.

When negotiations failed and the bank robber ignored the tearful pleas of his own detective father, police had no choice. They popped teargas, smoke and "flash bang" concussion grenades as they charged the house. WDAF listeners heard it all.

When the smoke cleared and Young was in custody, there stood John Wagner in the middle of the action.

It was quite a day. A bank was robbed, a police car was shot up, a news car was fired on, and a radio reporter had provided some heart-stopping coverage. Professor John Wagner had just taught another class in Radio News Reporting 101 to his helpless competitors.

WDAF·AM

SKY SPY

**John Wagner
Sky Spy Traffic**

FLY with the SKY SPY!

During the daily trek to and from work, Kansas City's largest listening audience tunes in to John Wagner, "Sky Spy", for traffic reports, alternate route suggestions and light-hearted barbs aimed at problem drivers. After twenty years of flying above rush-hour traffic, John Wagner is truly the dean of area traffic reporting.

Over the years, John Wagner, "Sky Spy," has earned many honors and citations for his service to the driving public. His most recent honors came on July 22 when The Safety and Health Council of Western Missouri & Kansas honored him for saving a life.

For Sky Spy availabilities and rates, call your 61 Country WDAF
Sales Representative 816-931-6100

Chapter 12

JOHN, THE STORM CHASER

SINCE JOHN CUT HIS TEETH on tornadoes in Wichita where most of them are hatched, he paid close attention to the killer storms when they threatened Kansas City.

He was in Overland Park, Kansas when a twister roared through a neighborhood and tore the roof off the Katherine Carpenter School. The storm struck at mid-afternoon when many of the children were already on buses in the school drive-way. Sam Bliss, a quick-thinking teacher, got them off the buses and back into the building where they huddled in a cove as the storm went past. No child was seriously hurt that day. John reported that.

On May 4, 1977, a day of tornadoes, Wagner spent most of the afternoon chasing twisters. The first one hit in early afternoon at Pleasant Hill, Missouri, which in the mid-1990s became the home base of the Severe Storms Forecast Center. Pleasant Hill was at ground zero that day. The tornado killed several people, hurt dozens more and tore several neighbor-hoods to pieces.

Wagner was the first Kansas City reporter to reach Pleas-ant Hill. The ambulances from Kansas City, Lee's Summit and Independence had not arrived yet. A lone Missouri State High-way Patrol trooper stood at the north end of town and told John he was free to go anywhere he wanted.

John quickly determined that the grade school at the north end of Pleasant Hill was badly damaged, but no children were there. He found them in another school at the town's southern edge. He broadcast that information repeatedly over WDAF to assure terrified parents that their youngsters were safe.

Wagner pointed out that another teacher was a hero that day, throwing himself over a group of children to shield them from falling debris, and suffered a serious leg injury in the process.

The situation in Pleasant Hill was under control in a short while, and television crews from Kansas City began arriving. It was time for the first reporter there to leave town.

As Wagner headed north, he heard reports of further tornado trouble, this time at Missouri City, a small town northeast of Kansas City on the banks of the Missouri River. He headed directly for Missouri City and broadcast confirmation of a tornado strike. Missouri City was luckier than Pleasant Hill. No one was killed, and any injuries were minor.

When he had wrapped up the Missouri City story, John heard radio traffic indicating tornado damage in Excelsior Springs, farther north in Clay County. John hurried there in time to broadcast the live sounds of rifle shots, as farmers disposed of their storm-injured hogs and other livestock. Damage to some buildings was heavy.

With only minutes of daylight left, the sun came out and the sky cleared. But that was not the end of it. The WDAF newsroom radioed John that Wyandotte and Johnson Counties in Kansas were under a tornado warning. He asked Caroline Rooney to confirm that report. She did, and seconds later Wagner was headed for Kansas.

Still not convinced a storm was out there, John changed his mind when he ran into a storm cell on I-435 at Kansas City's southern edge. It was a wall of heavy rain, complete with lightning, high wind and big hail.

He got through that and emerged in Olathe, where nothing seemed to be happening. It was time to step out of the car and grab a cigarette. As he did so, he broadcast a report that Olathe was quiet, very quiet, in fact, entirely too quiet. For, as he looked up, still broadcasting live on WDAF, he saw clouds starting to form a circle, a moving circle. He knew what that meant. The cloud mass drew itself together and came to ground just east of where John was standing. He jumped back into the news car and headed east on Highway 150, which is 135th Street. On the air all the way, he was describing the wind, the hail and the torrential rain, and said he could see silhouetted against the lightning the familiar tree trunk form of a tornado on the ground. He was about 250 feet north of it and running alongside it. Fortunately, the twister stayed on a due east course and never turned northeast as they usually do. That saved his life.

This writer was in another WDAF News car about half a mile behind John and could see people running from their homes and diving into ditches. They were all listening to what turned out to be yet another very dramatic high point in John Wagner's broadcasting career.

John had no way of knowing at the time that the tornado he was chasing had already touched down in parts of Olathe, causing millions of dollars in damage and hurting several people. It went back into the sky and then came down again near where John was having that cigarette.

The storms finally went away that night, ending a nearly 14-hour rampage of tornadoes.

Nobody ever forgot May 4, 1977. Most in the area knew well what to do when the warning sirens sounded. Take cover and tune in WDAF Radio (as long as John Wagner was still with the station).

The tornado season passed, and the fall flood season arrived early in September with a vengeance. On September 12 the Kansas City area was hit by the biggest one-day rainfall in its history. Early in the day six inches of rain fell, rapidly filling creeks and rivers and saturating the ground. That night another seven-inch rainfall was recorded, causing the biggest flood problem for Kansas City since the disastrous 1951 flood of the Missouri and Kaw Rivers.

WDAF Radio had broadcast all the flood watches and warnings issued by the National Weather Service. Still, no one could imagine what was about to happen that night.

John Wagner was on the streets all night, reporting live as Turkey Creek went on a rampage along Southwest Boulevard, wiping out several businesses. He watched and reported as Brush Creek, flowing through the fashionable Country Club Plaza, sent water into the shops and restaurants, flooding the streets, sweeping cars away like toys. He watched and reported as the Blue River rose out of its banks on the city's east side, wiping out houses and businesses and destroying hundreds of cars parked outside the General Motors plant in the Leeds District.

John stayed on the job all night and added to the work of the WDAF News staff working at the station and at several of the major emergency sites.

When daylight came, parts of the area looked like a war zone. Twenty-five people had been killed. Seventeen of those were trapped in cars, despite warnings not to drive through water.

Property damage was in the millions of dollars. Kansas City's pride and joy, the famous Plaza, was mud-scarred and littered with debris, trees, cars and, in some cases, human bodies.

Another casualty of the record rainstorms was Kansas City's feeling of security. No longer would anyone believe that Brush Creek was just a harmless stream through the Johnson County suburbs into the Plaza. It was no longer pretty. It was a killer and would have to be considered that in the future.

John Wagner's role in covering the dramatic events of September 12 and 13 is legendary. He demonstrated once again that radio is a very important link between public safety agencies and the public.

But that is true only as long as operators of radio stations have the right commitment and the right people to perform as grown-up, responsible members of the community.

It is a fact that few, if any, disc jockeys are remembered for their heroic work during the Kansas City floods of September 12 and 13, 1977.

Chapter 13

ONE MORE CLOSE CALL

IN A LIFE as active and near the edge as Wagner's, there have been some truly close calls.

One of these occurred one morning while he was flying over 75th and Ward Parkway in the south part of Kansas City. The gauges indicated the airplane, leased to WDAF, had lost oil pressure. That's serious.

As any veteran pilot would do, John had already chosen more than 20 fairly open spaces that could be used as emergency landing sites. Parks and golf courses were on his list.

From 75th and Ward Parkway, John turned the Cessna east and headed for his first choice: the Mall at Swope Park. When he got there, the engine was still turning. He decided to fly to his second choice, the Heart airstrip on Highway 40 in east Kansas City.

Once there, he noted the engine was still turning. He thought he might be able to reach his third choice, the levee along the Missouri River, not far from the airport. He turned north, and suddenly common sense took over. He decided to head back to the Heart and put the plane down on a runway.

Good decision. As he rolled to the end of the strip, the propeller locked up ... the engine had frozen. He would not have made it to the levee.

Wagner had talked with another pilot by radio during his crisis, insisting he was okay and would make it. But he wouldn't have, had he tried to fly much farther.

John flying over "his" town and "his" streets

The airplane, which had recently undergone a 100-hour inspection, had lost its oil because the safety wire had not been replaced on the engine oil plug.

John telephoned the company that owned the plane and reported the problem. "Not to worry," someone said. "We'll bring you a case of oil and you can fly it back to the airport."

In fairly blunt Wagner terms, John advised, "Somebody may fly that damned plane back to the airport, but it won't be me."

Chapter 14

MORE WAGNER ADVENTURES

BY THE 1970s the crime beat involved more than just cops and robbers. It included drugs and drug dealers. Police had to change their approach, and in cases had to go "undercover" and appear just like the scuzzy people they were tracking ... beards, long hair, earrings, peace medals, fringed clothing and the like.

One observer said the worst-looking ones had to be the cops ... self-respecting dope dealers couldn't afford to look that bad.

Federal and local investigators worked together, assembling all the information and intelligence they could gather and then deciding whether to go after the crooks at the local or federal level.

A good bit of this developed during the years John was in the theater business, away from broadcasting. And some procedures changed, too.

On one combined Clay and Platte County roundup of dopers, John was assigned to accompany a team of local and state lawmen. The arrest team arrived at a house and politely rang the doorbell. Getting no response, the officer said, "I guess there's no one at home."

John, remembering earlier times, said, "Stand back, let me handle this."

To the astonishment of the officers, Wagner kicked the door in. When an officer said, "We don't do things that way any more," John replied, "Well, you should. You'd accomplish a lot more."

Another huge narcotics investigation involved a man recognized as a high-ranking official in the Nation of Islam (the black Muslim movement) doubling as a heroin purveyor. Federal agents worked that case, built it and enlisted local and state officers to help bring it down.

Wagner noticed the unusual activity and men he didn't recognize gathering from time to time at the Kansas City police helicopter pad in east Kansas City. It was the assembly point and base of operations for the big raid. Wagner sniffed it out immediately and shared his new knowledge with the newsroom, swearing all to tight secrecy. The federal agents noticed him, too, and were terrified. They had long been taught to fear, hate and derail, where possible, the press. They were about to do that in this case, when some wise local officers pulled them aside and let them know that if any newsmen were to find out about the operation, the feds should appreciate the fact that it was discovered by Wagner and this writer instead of some of the flaky people working in other stations.

Preparations lasted for days and weeks. John code-named the investigators "the pavers," since competing radio and television stations, and even the *Kansas City Star,* monitored WDAF's two-way radio frequency. Those listening thought Wagner and his associates were talking about highway crews and never caught on to the real facts.

The day the operation finally came down, John Wagner, as usual, was alone among newsmen covering the story. And, of course, WDAF Radio had a long lead on the story, forcing the competitors either to steal the story directly from WDAF broadcasts, which some did regularly, or contact police and demand the information.

John's work in news coverage generally was warmly received by the listening audience. Where he caused sparks was in his traffic reporting. His favorite targets were slow drivers, Johnson County (Kansas) drivers, or anyone who happened to have a mechanical breakdown or run out of gas. John had no patience for people who slowed down his beloved traffic. He felt such sins should land someone in the electric chair. The complaints on John's broadcasts were nearly all on traffic. And everyone, it seemed, was listening. Some to admire and appreciate his work and others to loathe him for it.

When John and this writer went to the U.S. Secret Service office to pick up credentials for a presidential visit, the secretary asked for names. When they were mentioned, a side door was thrown open, and a dark-suited man came flying through that door, seized Wagner and pinned him against a wall, snarling, "Listen, you sonofabitch, lay off Johnson County drivers."

It was an agent who, when he was not accompanying Henry Kissinger or the President around the world, lived in Johnson County and worked out of the Kansas City office. In a moment it was funny. But for an instant John was not sure what was going on.

Indeed, nearly everybody listened when Wagner spoke. Emergency agencies kept track of WDAF's efforts, too. They monitored the two-way radio frequency, and one police department (Lenexa, Kansas) even cross-banded WDAF's frequency, so the station's newsmen and Lenexa dispatchers could talk to each other.

The Kansas City Fire Department listened, too. That was clear one evening when fire broke out on upper floors of a tall apartment building on Linwood Boulevard, near Forest. Deputy Chief Charles Fisher was in charge of the entire department that day.

Wagner, flying over the burning building before the first fire companies got there, radioed: "Charley, you're going to need a second alarm on this one." Immediately, the fire dispatchers sounded the call for a second alarm. They took John's word for it.

Wagner was generally on the side of the police and firemen. One day, however, he was not. He intercepted a police call sending Merriam, Kansas police to a market parking lot where a man had a "machine gun in the back seat of his car."

Before John and Merriam police could get there, the car started to move and headed down I-35, where it was quickly stopped by other officers. John was right behind them. When he ran up to the suspect car, officers quickly grabbed the machine gun, put it in a police car and raced away to Merriam Police Headquarters, ran inside and locked the doors.

The "machine gun" turned out to be a very real-looking plastic model of a Thompson .45 calibre sub-machine gun. (Old rule: When embarrassed and don't know how to explain, hide in the stationhouse and lock the doors.)

Many drivers went past the arrest scene, saw the flashing red lights on many police cars and saw a deadly looking weapon. An explanation would have been helpful. That's all John wanted. But that was apparently too much to ask that day of what John Wagner called "the one-antenna Merriam, Kansas Police Department."

Just one of a long list of memorable Wagnerisms.

As mentioned earlier, the successor to Clarence Kelley as police chief when Kelley because FBI director was not popular with the troops. He was not popular with John Wagner either.

Chief McNamara, to his credit, did try to fight crime in Kansas City. One of his efforts was a scheme, code-named Operation Robbery Control. It involved concentrating police officers near likely robbery targets, and went into operation the day after Thanksgiving, normally one of the busiest shopping days of the holidays.

The first day was a near tragedy. That morning as the stores opened, Officer Ramen Kerfoot, working downtown traffic, noticed a couple of thugs hurrying out of a jewelry store. When he tried to stop them, one turned and shot him in the chest at close range.

John, just two blocks away, got there seconds after Kerfoot hit the pavement. Newsman Wagner stood over him, helping others with first aid and broadcasting what had happened and offering a description of the getaway Cadillac.

John even mentioned that he was looking directly into the

the squire

gravely wounded policeman's face and spoke to him, getting a wink in response. He broadcast that, too, in case the man's wife was listening. "I wanted her to know, if she was hearing me, that her husband was still alive."

He was alive, but spent a long time recovering from the nearly fatal bullet wound. (Kerfoot recovered and spent his final years in uniform, with distinction, as a crew member in the police helicopter unit. He is now retired.)

The Wagner coverage of Kerfoot's very close call is well remembered when "real" policemen and "real" newsmen sit down to discuss how things happened in the "real" days.

Another incident involving the shooting of a policeman didn't end as well. There was nothing John Wagner could do to help Officer Russell Mestdagh on a cold winter day early in McNamara's Kansas City career.

The young patrolman was one of several dispatched to a drugstore holdup on 57th Street in south central Kansas City.

The officers secured the outside of the store and cautiously went inside, but not cautiously enough. One robber, still in the store, grabbed Mestagh from behind and shot him in the chest.

Wagner was furious. Someone had the nerve to kill a policeman. He regarded all policemen as friends (except for the very small handful who behaved like jerks). John was all over the crime scene and reported the story from every conceivable angle.

Chief McNamara was at the crime scene, too, vowing to go to Jefferson City to testify personally for restoration of the death penalty. He didn't go personally, but sent a high-ranking assistant to make the appeal. McNamara did the next best thing. He lobbied Kansas City businessmen for money to buy bullet-resistant vests. The early day body armor saved several lives in the subsequent months and years. And Joe McNamara deserves credit for that.

Over the years since then the question of body armor (mandatory or optional) has been debated at length.

The general consensus: as hot and bulky as it is, it is still more comfortable than a casket.

Chapter 15

TROUBLE WITH THE MAFIA

AS JOHN WAGNER CONTINUED his daily patrols on and above the streets of Kansas City, the neighborhood of ancient buildings in the City Market district, renamed River Quay, began to boom, literally.

Many saloons, cocktail lounges, nightclubs (some virtually "strip joints") opened for business, many of them underfinanced. This brought in some of the Mafia's loan sharks.

There was a shortage of parking space. This brought in some of the Mafia's killers.

John Wagner was all over this developing news story. It was clearly a war between the established Mafia organization and a dissident element.

It came to public attention on July 22, 1976, when Police Officers Curry Bates and Bruce Royce noticed thick red liquid dripping from the trunk of a black-over-green Mustang, abandoned at 9th and Olive. When they opened the trunk, they found the bullet-riddled body of David Bonadonna. His son, Freddie, who operated a joint in the Quay, had refused to give up some of his parking space to the established Mafia element.

John was there as the trunk was opened and was convinced the war was on. The FBI was convinced, too. G-men believed Bonadonna was killed in Willie Camissano's garage at 536 Monroe, and obtained a warrant to search the place. A federal judge granted the search warrant after getting an FBI affidavit which stated the agents expected to find "blood, particles of flesh, bone and hair, fibers from clothing, a .32 caliber automatic pistol, expended bullets, shell casings and bullet-damaged furniture and other property."

The FBI was quick, but not quick enough. Willie's garage was clean, scrubbed clean.

As John Wagner observed, "This isn't over yet."

A month later, August 25, a Jackson County Grand Jury assembled to study the mob war. That Grand Jury was about as successful in investigating the politically savvy Mafia as all the other Jackson County grand juries over the years. No indictments.

John Wagner continued to search for other developments. It didn't take long. In late September Joe Camissano's dance joint in the Quay was fire damaged. The next day a pipe bomb went off at the Columbus Park Social Club on East 5th. It as better known as the Trap, where the Mafia hierarchy regularly met and plotted.

The next Mafia murder to be covered was in a KCI airport parking lot. The body of John Brocato, tortured, mutilated, then frozen, was in a car trunk. John Wagner was there.

More retaliation in February of 1977. John Amaro, also known as Johnny Green, was shot to death in his garage in the Northland. This broke two long-standing rules in the Mafia code of decency. Never "hit" a man in his own home. And never "hit" a man a mere block from the home of the local Mafia boss, Nick Civella.

Three days later, February 22nd, Harold "Sonny" Bowen was in a midtown joint called "Mr. O'Brien's" at Armour and Broadway. Sonny didn't know it, but he was having his last drink, and his last breath. The bartender, polishing glasses, turned away and didn't see the three Mafia killers enter and go right to Bowen's booth. It was over in seconds.

Though there would be other Mafia killings in the years ahead, the only unfinished business in the current squabble concerned one man who didn't have long to live, and John Wagner knew it.

Gary T. Parker, a heavy drinker who moved from saloon

to saloon, refused FBI offers of protection and said he could take care of himself. Gary was wrong.

Gary, also known was Parker T., was in an east side saloon at Truman Road and Jackson Friday afternoon, August 5th, 1977. Parker T. was having what would be his last drink. John Wagner was in the airplane, covering the early part of the afternoon traffic rush. Police Officer Curtis Welch was driving his paddy wagon west on Truman Road heading for downtown police headquarters.

Gary Parker finished that last drink and walked out the door toward his car on the parking lot just west of the building. He was beside his car when the bomb was set off by remote control.

At that instant the police wagon rolled past, and Welch heard the heavy boom and saw a human arm, hand attached, strike his windshield and then splatter on a white concrete building across the street. The shocked Welch quickly called the police dispatcher and reported an explosion at Truman and Jackson.

At the same instant John Wagner was directly overhead and heard Officer Welch's emergency call. He was on the air immediately and said: "Police report an explosion at Truman and Jackson. I'm directly overhead and don't see a thing. They must be mistaken. No, wait a minute. I now see smoke starting to rise from the parking lot. Yes, there was indeed an explosion down there, and it was a big one."

Wagner flew the plane back to Signal Hill and flew above this writer on his way out there, to offer him a fast way to reach the bombing scene. Knowing which stop signs it was safe to violate was a big help.

The bomb murder of Gary Parker was carried out on a Friday afternoon, John's final day before vacation.

The following week, police called the newsroom looking for him. One woman who said she witnessed the explosion swore the bomb was dropped from John Wagner's airplane. He was on his sailboat on Lake of the Ozarks and out of reach of a telephone.

His response to that suggestion: "I've done a lot of crazy things in my life, but I have never dropped a bomb from the airplane."

The killing of Gary Parker ended only one phase of the Mafia war. There were still three surviving Spero brothers to kill. They were. Then Mike Kattou was killed in an Independence Avenue body shop, and Andy Mancuso was found in his car south of the Plaza.

Then the shooting stopped. And John Wagner had other major news stories to cover.

Chapter 16

WAGNER, THE CELEBRITY

THOUGH IT HASN'T BEEN directly mentioned yet, John rapidly became a "personality on the radio station.

That is a term usually reserved for the disc jockeys, since their role is strictly entertainment (though many of them are intellectually poorly equipped for the assignment).

John, bearing the station-assigned title Sky Spy, rode on

floats in parades, performed aerial stunts in circuses and made personal visits to area schools and organizations.

He was a major attraction for WDAF along routes of the annual American Royal and St. Patrick's Day parades. He would quickly tire of being confined on a float, would jump off and run along beside the vehicle, shaking hands and personally greeting "fans" along the way.

At one circus he recalls being fitted with "wings" and helmet and goggles, a harness, attached to cables and being suddenly pulled out of his seat in the audience and hoisted high above the arena floor. He was pulled back and forth as though flying. All the while the ring announcer was describing his "flight" over the crowd. The circus goers loved it, and so did John.

He was fearless, and that included not being afraid of what anyone thought of him. One day when making a personal appearance at a suburban high school, which included speaking to a class, John noticed that one teen-aged boy was paying no attention and was being a smart aleck. It was easily handled. When the teacher ignored the problem, John ordered the boy out of the room. (He has always had an allergy to punks.)

He was frequently outspoken in his broadcast work. He had little use for earrings or long hair on males, or any other forms of stupidity. He had little use for politicians. He named several of the viaducts and ancient bridges in Kansas City for former and current office-holders, reasoning that, like their human namesakes, the bridges were old, unreliable, rusting, crumbling and in danger of collapse.

He never met Will Rogers and was never mistaken for Dale Carnegie or Mother Teresa. He was, and still is, John Wagner.

John was always aware of the impact of on-the-scene radio reporting. Getting there was sometimes of secondary importance to being there.

When he was enroute to a fire and the sound of sirens was passing by, he held the mike out the window and verbally imagined what it must be like at the scene. Sometimes the line between being there and enroute became a little blurred.

Bill Ellingsworth, a man with a great deal of experience in news coverage, remembers just such an event. Bill, then a reporter for the *Kansas City Times,* the morning *Kansas City Star,* was dispatched late one night, very near a "deadline," to a major jail riot in a suburban county. The City Desk radioed, asking Bill where he was and added that he had better hurry, because John Wagner was already on the scene and "killing" the newspaper with broadcast details.

Bill radioed back: "The hell he is. I'm right behind him on the highway. And we're both doing about 80."

"With that I tuned him in on the radio and, sure enough, he was giving a very convincing on-the-scene report (from the highway). You gotta love it. With that note, I should say I covered many stories with John over the years — both as a newsman and as a member of the police department — and always found John to be a solid and innovative reporter."

That's a hefty endorsement from a man of Ellingsworth's background. He left the *Kansas City Times* to become media aide to Clarence Kelley in the Kansas City Police Chief's office.

When Kelley was named FBI director, Bill Ellingsworth moved to Washington with him in the same capacity.

Today Ellingsworth is Senior Staff Vice President for Public Affairs for the National Association of Homebuilders in its Washington headquarters. He still remembers battling John Wagner to be first at breaking news stories on the streets of Kansas City .

Sky Spy gets safety honor

By The Star's staff

A month ago, the Federal Aviation Admininstration was all over Sky Spy John Wagner of WDAF-AM. The agency cited Wagner for violating five regulations, including operating an aircraft "in a careless manner so as to endanger the life or property of another."

John Wagner

On Monday, he was given kudos by the Safety and Health Council of Western Missouri and Kansas for saving a life.

At the group's 11th annual safety awards luncheon, Wagner was among six persons honored for lifesaving, said Mike Costello, vice president and general manager of the radio station.

Others honored by the council were Jeffrey Carson and Dr. Melvin D. Karges, for assisting at a vehicle accident; Adam Scott, for helping a fellow window washer to safety after an accident; John J. Vogel Jr., for saving a child about to be hit by a runaway car; Kevin Gunderson, a 6-year-old who sought help during a boating accident with his grandfather; and Harold Knabe, Kansas City Fire Department spokesman, for his years of service.

In the wee hours of Feb. 19, Wagner broadcast a report of a high-speed chase taking place in eastern Jackson County involving a stolen vehicle and police. A driver who was about to turn into the path of the chase stopped and pulled over to the curb just as the suspect zoomed past.

He wrote a letter to the council crediting Wagner with his life, Costello said.

The award doesn't cancel his record with the FAA. The case still is pending.

Chapter 17

FIRE!

ONE OF THE MANY BIG FIRES John will never forget was in the west bottoms.

The fire in the Superior Toy Company was already a multi-alarm incident when John got there on a blustery cold afternoon. The flamboyant deputy fire chief, Benny Imperiale, was in command. He and Wagner decided to get a closer look at the inside of the burning building and instead got an unplanned adventure.

At first glance it appeared that the stuffing used in plush toys (bits of foam) was standing several feet deep in a large room. It was, but it was already mixed with several feet of water from the fire hoses. Before they realized what they were into, both chief and newsman were literally swimming in the mixture and had to fight their way back to "dry land."

John recalls the building was a concrete structure with heavy foot-square wooden beams, complete with a concrete roof. This served to "seal" in the fire and make it very intense.

All this was being broadcast on WDAF over John's walkie talkie radio. He reported Chief Imperiale's decision to use an explosive charge to punch a hole in the solid roof to allow ventilation. But how do you "bomb" a building to fight a fire? No problem for the resourceful Benny Imperiale. He ordered a fireman to carry an explosive pack up an aerial, extended out over the roof of the building. He did as ordered, placed the pack on the roof and scampered down the aerial to safety.

Seconds later, the "bomb" went off, and out the new hole in the roof came a geyser of water, smoke, fire and a large plume of toy stuffing material. That broke the back of the fire, and before long it was under control. It wasn't the first damaging fire at Superior Toy, or the last. All that was left for the Kansas City Fire Department was the paper work and cleaning up the equipment.

All that was left for John Wagner was explaining to the WDAF engineers what had happened to the expensive walkie talkie radio that got soaked when he fell face down in nearly a foot of water at the big fire. He didn't mind what happened to the radio, but his pride was damaged when forced to admit that he, John Wagner, had fallen.

John's reports were heard over a wide area that day. WDAF received a letter a few days later from a man, fascinated by John's coverage, while driving through Kansas City. He asked permission to use some of Wagner's material in a book he was writing on urban disasters. Permission was granted.

John had another adventure in nearly the same part of town a few years later when the firefighters union went on strike. Such a strike was an arsonist's dream.

Firebugs were waiting when night came. Their first fire was set in a vacant warehouse in the bottoms. John was there, doing what he always did, standing right in front of the burning building and describing it on the air.

What John didn't know was that other fire departments had pledged to assist Kansas City. One of these was Gladstone, which in those days had a combined police/fire, or Public Safety Department. This meant that Gladstone firefighters were also police officers.

As a big Gladstone fire truck pulled in behind John, the man in charge realized he needed to ventilate the building.

John's reports were always full of excitement, but were especially so that night when Gladstone firemen used their police shotguns to open up the burning building. They were behind him, but fortunately were well above him. In a few minutes his heart beat returned to a more normal level.

On a bitterly cold Saturday morning in late January 1978, the historic Coates House Hotel on the corner of 10th and Broadway caught fire. Though the old building had fallen into disrepair and disrepute over the years, it had been, in better days, a "must" stop for anyone who was anyone, including the President of the United States. Grover Cleveland may have been the first. The building was under construction when the Civil War broke out. Horses were stabled in its unfinished basement.

By 1978, the Coates House was no longer a distinguished address. It was home only to those who could afford to live nowhere else. This included pensioners, some of them disabled, and an assortment of drunks and "unregistered guests."

The temperature was not far above zero that morning. Fire trucks became locked in ice in the street. Public Works trucks were brought in to spread salt and bull-dozers to break up the "icebergs" on the pavement. But that wasn't the story that morning.

The real story involved far more than ice and cold weather. Only God knows how many people were killed in the fire. The only numbers known to man vary from 20 to 25.

When John arrived at the fire, he remembered that he had spent the night in the Coates House on his first visit to

KMBC. He could still recall the layout of the vintage building, which helped as he mingled with the police, firemen and body retrieval teams. He was literally all over the building, even on floors where it was still quite dangerous. One man made it to a window, just inches from rescue, and fell back into the flames. Another lost consciousness while waiting for rescue at a window ledge and was draped over it when an aerial truck broke down, leaving the lifeless body encased in ice, in clear view of the street for several days.

All these incidents were broadcast dramatically from inside and outside the old hotel by Wagner. He stepped out of the building to catch a whiff of smoke-free air just as a man fell or jumped from a third-story window, caught a beam with one arm and dropped to the sidewalk. His arm was nearly severed, but he was alive.

When John scrambled into the ambulance to catch a quick interview with the lucky man, he quickly realized why the man had survived, later commenting: "A sober man would have been killed."

He went back into the building for more live broadcasts. He called on the radio to this writer: "Hey, Charley, look up here, on the sixth floor." There he was in the bare window frame, 60 feet above the street. Little of the wall remained around him. Behind him lay several bodies, which he described for the WDAF audience so the public would know what kind of Hell the fire had been.

By now, daylight was trying to establish itself. The first rays of the sun cut through the remaining smoke and the heavy frost. As John stood there with many bodies on the floor behind him, he saw the sun hit the gold roof and the cross atop the Cathedral of the Immaculate Conception, a block from the tragedy. Perhaps it was a brief flashback to the teaching of those humorless nuns at St. Henry's school in Chicago that prompted him to say on WDAF: "When I see that cathedral and that cross, I wonder if that's the last thing some of these people saw. I believe it was."

The fire was out. The investigation was begun. Dangerous parts of the Coates House were torn down. In a few years it would reopen and would be a much safer and nicer, though smaller, place.

The Coates House fire tragedy was the first of three major fires in Kansas City. The next day, Sunday morning, the Brookside Theater burned. John was not there. But the following day, Monday, when fire developed in the Twin Oaks Apartments at 50th and Oak, he was there in fine form.

He raced through the multi-story twin buildings, with firemen and police. Hundreds of people were rescued and led to safety that morning. Firefighters had breathing equipment. Police did not, and several of them collapsed while rescuing elderly people. John, keeping up a drumfire of broadcast reports from inside the huge smoky building, saw that a police friend, Sgt. Joe Coulson, needed some oxygen. He was barely conscious as John pulled alongside him. Wagner called for help. Coulson was taken by ambulance to a hospital, where a heart problem was discovered.

The emergency was handled with a minimum of civilian casualties, the fire was extinguished, and the fire department's investigation was launched. Some changes in building safety were recommended.

Finally the temperature got back to a more comfortable range, and buildings stopped burning ...for a while.

When you covered as many incidents as Wagner had, you had a pretty fair idea what you'd be facing when you got to the scene. That experience, coupled with his understanding of how things worked, gave him a great advantage. He also had an almost poetic ability to put his finger right on the essence of a situation.

One late afternoon, while covering traffic downtown, he hurried to an intersection where a blind man with a guide dog had been hit by a city bus. The poor fellow was trapped beneath the bus, and the faithful dog would not allow anyone near his master. Wagner's description: "If you've ever seen anguish in a dog's face, you see it now at 9th and Baltimore."

On a far less serious occasion, a Kansas City visit by President Jimmy Carter, Wagner was held outside a Brooklyn Avenue barbecue shop while the President was inside, sampling "beef and an RC."

The descriptive juices began to flow again, turning Wagner's attention to the crowd of spectators. On WDAF, and with a straight face, he described "a little lady, telling a small poodle she was holding: "See, Binky, I told you the President would come to see us today."

To this day no one really knows whether such a little lady or a dog named Binky ever existed. But it was a bit more interesting than a description of President Carter wiping Arthur Bryant's sauce off the First chin.

John receiving a life-saving award from Tom Cox, Board Chairman of the Safety and Health Council of Western Missouri and Kansas.

Chapter 18

RESCUE FROM THE RIVER

FOR HIGH DRAMA blended with outstanding radio reporting, it would be impossible to top December 9, 1975, on the Paseo Bridge.

At mid-morning the music suddenly stopped, and the recorded introduction to a WDAF News bulletin was played.

"This is John Wagner approaching the Paseo Bridge. Police report someone has just jumped into the river. Traffic is nearly stopped, a police helicopter is circling, and many people are slowing down to gawk. A small VW is parked on the bridge, the Fire Department is launching a boat in Riverfront Park, and I'll be back in a minute with details of the search for the victim's body."

A few minutes later, Wagner came back on the air from the bridge floor. "This guy hasn't jumped, and if police have their way, he won't. He is a young fellow, pretty good-sized, wearing blue jeans, no shoes or socks, a blue and white striped shirt. He is below the bridge floor on a narrow platform just at the middle pier of the bridge. He has a beard and long hair, has laid out his money, perhaps all his worldly possessions, and he's ready to end it."

John continued his live broadcast description: "He is about ten feet below me, and I can hear police trying to talk to him. But when they get too close, he moves toward the edge. He couldn't hit the water from here, but he would hit concrete footings about 80 feet below. It's extremely cold here, but fortunately there is not much wind."

Sgt. Dick Hoedl, who had taken hours of psychology classes, was nearest the distraught young man. Hoedl's voice can be heard on tapes of the incident: "Look at me, listen to me. There are hundreds of routes you can take. You can always come back and do this if you have to, but you haven't tried everything else."

Later Hoedl would say: "We talked to him. We told him we'd try to help him. He said dying was the only way he had left."

Hoedl, a second-generation Kansas City policeman, tried every trick in the book that say. Several times in the incident that lasted for hours, Wagner would refer to Hoedl as Leo. (Leo, a retired police lieutenant, was Dick Hoedl's father).

A Fire Department captain joined the effort. John Wagner noted that someone had tied a slipknot in the lifeline that was about to be wrapped around Hoedl's waist. Wagner warned the team that such a knot would pull tight and literally cut the sergeant in half. He suggested a bowline knot, whose loop is knotted firmly in place if tied correctly. They handed him the rope, and John Wagner, ex-scoutmaster and sailboat sailor, tied it.

Wagner resumed the broadcast: "Hoedl has him by the hair, another officer is reaching for his foot. They're lowering another rope (adding his own suggestion): put a loop in it, and we'll try to drop it around the guy's legs. There's only enough room for one man to work down there. The ledge is less than four feet wide, and even though Hoedl is trying to pull the man back, there's nothing to hang onto. Hoedl is still trying to hold the man, but he's breaking loose and kicking at the policeman. Hoedl is holding him with one hand. They're trying to save this guy, but he won't help. Hoedl is lying on that narrow platform, and still they can't get the man under control."

Then Wagner's role as a reporter was interrupted. "Another bowline? Okay. They want me to tie another knot. I'll be back on the air in a few minutes." And he put the walkie talkie down on the bridge.

Back on the air three minutes later, Wagner said, "They're taking a break. Hoedl has lit a cigarette for himself and the man he's trying to save. Though smoking can be dangerous to your health, in this case, it's kind of a respite."

The struggle resumed. "They have him handcuffed, but they still have to get him to the bridge floor level, and he's still fighting them. He's screaming. He's lost his shirt in the struggle, his flesh is raw and red from both the cold and being brushed against those golf-ball-sized rivet heads. Now the police are wrapping several ropes around him."

And then it ended. "They've got him now and are lifting him up that small ladder. Even now, he's not helping them. But they feel good. They have kept this guy from killing himself. It was a textbook operation."

The police wrapped up their part of it by slamming the paddy wagon doors and sending it off to the Psychiatric Receiving Center.

John Wagner, swinging in space with one foot on the bridge and holding to a bridge cable with only one arm, closed it out this way: "Thank you, Dick Hoedl. They could have lost the man, lost two policemen and a fire captain, but they didn't. It's all over on the Paseo Bridge. This is John Wagner, WDAF News."

Months later, when WDAF submitted tapes of Wagner's outstanding work that day to the Radio Television News Directors Association annual competition, the entry was returned and noted: "The judges could not agree on the advisability of giving news coverage to a suicide attempt."

Author's note: The judges were at Pullman, Washington, which suggests they were journalism professors and/or students.

Additional footnote: Two years later, still a young man, Sgt. Dick Hoedl, hero, second-generation Kansas City policeman, died of cancer.

Chapter 19

SKY SPY

JOHN WAS actually living two lives. He was flying the WDAF traffic spotter airplane morning and afternoon, using the company title Sky Spy. And in between flights was covering street news of the ground as only he could.

Though his ground news work was spectacular, the remarks he made while reporting on traffic generated the most public reaction. He offended Johnson County drivers, whom he assumed were all dumb. He offended anyone whose car broke down, assuming they had stupidly run out of gas.

One day a highly agitated citizen telephoned WDAF from a pay phone on I-70, demanding John Wagner's head. "Wagner said on the radio the idiot driving that yellow VW down there on I-70 had better get that heap off the road. I heard him while driving my yellow VW on I-70. Please fire him."

One morning at the end of his traffic flight, John heard fire alarms in a large agricultural chemical plant in far northeast Kansas City. The operators of that plant ruled that no newsman, and very few firemen, will ever get beyond the gates. No problem: John flew circles around the plant in the Sky Spy airplane and gave colorful descriptions of the big firefight going on below.

He covered the story on radio while his competitors were listening and gnashing their teeth at the security gates. The mother of a radio station employee, working as a chemist in the plant, later told her daughter that John's broadcasts were heard all over the plant, and he gave the employees better information than the company did.

John used the same tactics at Armco Steel and other outfits that had "no news" rules. He said: "I'll cover the news any way I have to, with or without their cooperation."

John and that airplane could cover floods, too, even when those in charge denied there were any levee breaches. One morning, after hearing reports from citizens and official denials of any problems, John flew downstream over the Missouri River and found six levee breaks, even though officialdom was saying the river is high, but the levees are holding.

Two days later, after his repeated reports, the official story was changed, proving again that it was hard to fool a man who could see what was really happening.

John Wagner made penetrating the boundaries of police barricade situations a way of life. He liked being able to broadcast from inside the lines and as close as possible to the real action.

One evening when a gunman got inside the General Motors assembly plant in the Leeds district and took a couple of hostages, police responded in their usual manner, and John offered to carry a police sniper's rifle, just to get into the plant, of course.

Once inside, Wagner began broadcasting live reports on WDAF. When, in places, his walkie talkie was unable to penetrate the steel walls of the factory, he used plant telephones. That was his downfall.

Factory officials, both at home and at work, were hearing the reports and were disturbed that a member of the news media could get past security officers. The word to security was: "Get that guy out of there."

One guard caught John using a pay telephone in an employee lounge area and grabbed him. John turned to him and said: "I'll do what you say and go where you say to go, but don't you put a hand on me."

To expedite his ejection, security guards put John on an electric cart and rolled him to the front gate. He broadcast live, protesting his expulsion from a big news story.

Only when this writer advised him, outside the plant, that he was really trespassing, did John calm down.

Back to the story. The gunman was aiming directly at the head of a woman hostage and was beginning to squeeze the trigger when the police commander ordered his sniper to take the gunman down. Done. Headshot.

The police sniper later became a sergeant, and years later was killed in a motorcycle crash. Wagner carried his rifle that night.

John's activities rolled on at a hectic pace. He was kept quite busy flying the airplane and covering traffic during peak traffic periods in morning and afternoon. In between flights he covered breaking news from his car on the ground.

The ground coverage was consistently always exciting. The traffic coverage from the air was what attracted the most public attention ... and controversy. John was, to put it mildly, outspoken. He came to regard the traffic flow as his personal property. And woe to any driver who made a careless mistake and complicated things.

In the late 1970s when farmers were lining up in so-called tractorcades to deliver their complaints to Washington, a long line of expensive, powerful but slow-moving conveyances rolled through Kansas City during the evening rush hour. John was watching from overhead and was outraged to see "his" traffic flow tangled by the tractors.

He was not very tactful.

The farmers, already angry over low farm prices and frequent foreclosure when loan collateral values slumped, became even angrier when they heard what they had considered their favorite radio station hammering them for messing up traffic. Most of the farm rigs had telephones, which the farmers used to complain to the radio station.

Chastened for his remarks, John stuck basically to his guns because, in his world, good traffic flow was holy and sacred.

Another similar situation developed when runners began

carrying the Olympic Torch through town. John was overhead in the early morning and didn't appreciate it at all when "those durn fools pranced out there on busy highways, even with police escorts, and got in the way and messed up traffic."

This also produced some complaints from the listening public, but John remained unrepentant. "They had no right to get in the way of traffic. And besides, streets are made to move traffic, not to park on."

The annual lighting of the famous Country Club Plaza Christmas Lights has been a Thanksgiving night tradition in Kansas City for years. John was assigned to fly over the scene and broadcast a description when the lights came on. His treatment of the subject was as colorful as the lights themselves. "There they go! The reds, the blues, the greens, the yellows, the whites. Nothing has ever been more beautiful than this. Oh, you should see the Plaza lights the way I see them!"

It was another side of John Wagner, a side the motoring public seldom heard. No magic in that ... John merely called them the way he saw them.

John has always had a special place in his heart for trees. He could be as eloquent when describing the fall colors of trees as he flew about them as he was in covering the Christmas light of the city.

He often said cemeteries are the prettiest places in town because they have the prettiest trees ... especially in autumn. The trees in those places seem to get more tender loving care than their counterparts, left to shift for themselves along streets and alleyways.

One of Wagner's choice assignments one day was to cover the arrival in the city of the Mayor's Christmas Tree. Such a tree is always a very tall one, cut in some other part of the country and brought to Kansas City on a flatbed trailer. Such a long rig requires a police motorcycle escort.

John was faithfully tracking the 60-footer in his news car when he became tangled in some traffic and lost sight of the trailer and escorts. He briefly panicked, then recovered in typical Wagner fashion, urging his listeners to be on the lookout for the missing Christmas Tree. "Follow any clues you can find such as broken green branches, or better yet, pine cones. I frankly don't want to become the first broadcast traffic reporter in history to lose a 60-foot tree. Help me!" No one did. But the Mayor's tree made it safely to its Crown Center destination and served its purpose, without John's assistance.

He loved parades, especially the annual American Royal parade staged on the first really cold Saturday morning in November. John, being a free spirit, could accept confinement on the radio station's float only so long. When he could stand it no longer, he bounded off the trailer and began running alongside the procession, shaking hands and greeting friends and strangers alike. No politician ever worked a crowd better than he did.

But as happy and active as everything seemed to be, those old familiar storm clouds began to appear again. John could feel them even before he could see them. His personal relationship with those running the radio station was beginning to fray.

It was apparent in little ways. Frequent criticism over unimportant matters, nitpicking supervision from those minor supervisors whose understanding of real broadcasting came from books instead of experience, and worst of all, increased mechanical problems with the airplane he was assigned to fly. He found that his complaints about the new problems were not really being supported by those who should have been looking out for him.

All these added up to an uneasy feeling that the old signs of trouble from the past were coming back.

Chapter 20

MORE CHALLENGES FOR JOHN

WHEN TROUBLE CAME, John usually immersed himself in a couple of very distracting hobbies — gardening and sailing. John had begun keeping gardens in the early days of his broadcasting career in Wichita.

When he and Helen bought what was to be their longtime family home in east Kansas City, John set up an elaborate backyard that could have been featured on a garden magazine cover. He built a 20 x 40-foot garden. It included raised beds, a small greenhouse and flowers that attracted every type of bird or butterfly ever seen in this part of the country. Of course, there were vegetables, including tomatoes which he doesn't like. But one would never know that from the loving care he gave them.

Then he dug a 10 x 20-foot pond, surrounded it with appropriate plants and stocked it with big goldfish. The birds, drawn by John's flowers, and the goldfish in the pond were certainly tempting to the neighborhood cats. Just one problem for them though — John's big Doberman Pinscher. The cats wisely settled for standard cat food at home.

Next he built an arched bridge over the pond. It was a dandy and capped the entire project very artfully.

When everything in the backyard was done and nothing else required his attention, John drove to Lake Jacomo where his sailboat, Vicarious, was moored. His interest and zest for sailing had been with him a long time.

Years earlier, while working in Wichita, John was invited by the Navy to get to Olathe and catch a flight to Newport News, Virginia to cover the christening of the U.S.S. Enterprise.

One of his seatmates was Ted Rice, who was not only a weekend sailor but also a cameraman for a Kansas City television station. Ted told John of the joys and challenges of sailing. John, interested in both joy and challenge, quickly jumped into sailing when he arrived in Kansas City sometime later.

He acquired a 21-footer with a cabin and became quite active on the water. John picked up navigational skills and in no time at all could sail, maneuver and tie knots with the best of them. He later described sailing, especially the navigation part, as being very much like flying. No doubt he enjoyed the challenges and the risk taking of both.

Strange as it may seem to most people, accustomed to comfort and the relative safety of their homes, John was not a fair weather sailor. Oh, he sailed in nice weather and enjoyed it, but he really preferred to handle his boat in stormy conditions. His philosophy: "Any durned fool can sail a boat when the weather is nice, but it takes a real sailor to handle one of the things in a storm.

He proved that on many occasions. He sailed a boat in very much the same manner as he flew airplanes. He wanted to test himself at all times by seeing how close to the edge he could get, whether in the air or on the water. And he liked to test the endurance of his vehicle, whether airplane or sailboat.

On certain occasions he got too near the edge. One of these concerned a radio station-sponsored hot air balloon event at Richards-Gebaur Air Force Base. Dozens of balloons were poised to take part in the event, but had to wait because wind conditions weren't right. John's role was to fly over the base several times and broadcast to the crowd. A number of loudspeakers had been set up to carry all the sounds to the people there and those listening elsewhere to the radio station.

With the balloons briefly grounded, John was the only flying act of the event so far. It quickly became boring to him. He decided to make it a bit more exciting by looping the airplane. The crowd loved it, so he did it about six or seven more times. Few people had ever seen a Cessna 172 flying loops.

Though exciting to see, the stunt caused some serious trouble for John. First, the Cessna 172 is not rated for acrobatic flying. Second, several FAA inspectors were in the crowd. John's actions cost him a temporary pilot's license suspension. The station had to pay another licensed pilot to handle the plane for Wagner during the suspension.

On more than one occasion John would comment on the air just as he was landing the plane in particularly tough weather conditions, "Thank you, Mr. Cessna, for building a very forgiving airplane."

He knew how good it was, long before trying that touchy landing.

The one thing John never lacked, at least outwardly, was confidence in his own ability to handle any situation. This included handling a car on a high-speed news assignment, getting into or out of a tight spot, knowing just where to flop down and stay just out of the line of fire in a gun battle, knowing just which way a burning building would collapse, how to handle an airplane on a scary crosswind landing or a sailboat in rough water.

It was that confidence and a love for adventure that prompted John and Helen and several of their sailing buddies from Lake Jacomo to embark on a ten-day sailing cruise in the Virgin Islands.

After an air trip from the U.S. Mainland, the party arrived at Tortola, where a 44-foot sailboat had been reserved. The plan was to sail it 34 miles from Virgin Gorde, British Virgin Islands, to St. Croix, American Virgin Islands.

John plotted the course, and each member of the party had a turn at the wheel. John later explained that, even though the boat was rarely beyond the sight of land, it was still unfamiliar territory and would still give all aboard a test of navigational skills.

He proudly recalls hitting the exact target spot on St. Croix and sailing directly into Christiansted Harbor. Not bad for a crew whose only sailing and navigating experience was on a man-made lake in Jackson County, Missouri.

While on St. Croix Island, the crew swam, snorkeled, dived for conch (a shellfish and quite a delicacy) and enjoyed the white beaches. John developed a real appetite for conch. He found it everywhere, even at a Kentucky Fried Chicken stand. He bought a quantity of it and took it back to the sailboat for a feast.

How misleading short vacation visits to tropical paradises can be. The vacationer sees only the good things. The reality of it somehow isn't noticed.

A second trip to St. Croix was even more fascinating. John and Helen found a pizza shop with seating for 24 with living quarters upstairs. It seemed to be a nice spot. What's more, they learned the place was for sale.

Now he was really hooked. He thought of the increasingly unhappy situation at the radio station and how happy he and Helen could be, living in this paradise, far from disc jockeys, disc jockey program directors and a general manager who didn't seem to like him.

St. Croix appeared to be heaven on earth. (Far from it, as he would later learn.) Still, he couldn't get that place out of his mind. He kept seeing himself, Helen and their two dogs (Poodle and Doberman) and their car on the island, making a decent living selling pizza to the hungry masses. It didn't work out that way at all.

They agreed to go for it and made a deal to buy the pizza shop. They returned to Kansas City, announced their intentions, gave notice to WDAF and began packing.

The sailboat and several other possessions were sold. The only major holding not sold was their east-side house on Overton Circle. That turned out to be a very good decision.

The appropriate farewell parties were attended. The Kansas City Fire Department held a luncheon honoring John at Number Ten Station at 9th and Paseo. He was given a gold Battalion Chief Badge (number 61). That party was on Thursday. Friday morning, John's last day at WDAF, the firemen spread white powder on the parking lot in huge letters reading, "Good Luck, John." He could see it from the airplane.

The radio station gave John a Bearcat scanner, capable of picking up police, fire, emergency medical and marine communications as a farewell gift. He took it home at the end of his work day, quickly programmed it and continued packing.

That evening shortly after seven o'clock John heard his new scanner describing a horrible event at the Hyatt Regency Hotel, where the skywalks had fallen, killing more than 100 people.

He was seriously torn. Should he hustle down there and get involved in the news coverage? Should he stay home, since he had already resigned and left the station? The decision was not easy. He admitted later he was in and out of the door 17 times before he decided to let go and stay at home.

Having apparently severed his emotional ties to the news business in Kansas City (or so he thought) and mentally moved into the next phase in which he would be a pizza provider in the Virgin Islands, John completed packing.

The move actually began a few days later. It did not go smoothly. First there was a big argument with the airline, which considered the Wagner family Doberman entirely too big to ride in a commercial airliner. The much smaller Poodle was no problem, but both had to submit to being locked in cages for the long flight.

Helen decided to stop in Florida for a few days to visit their son, Jim, at a naval base. John and the canine entourage went ahead to St. Croix, where on arrival there was another transportation crisis. The cab driver bluntly informed Wagner that taxis did not transport dogs. That problem was solved, and John and dogs arrived at the pizza shop which was to be their new home.

The transportation problems with the dogs were omens of further trouble to come. For no sooner than John had obtained all the necessary paperwork, including health certificates, the red tape began to coil itself around the venture.

John thought he had seen everything in his dealings with

the petty bureaucrats in Kansas City. But he began to learn from the people who write and teach courses in bureaucracy. It is apparently a national sport in the Virgin Islands, especially when the victim of it comes from the mainland.

After more grief from local authorities and being closed down three times, John and Helen began to view St. Croix as a tropical paradise through a different lens. It didn't take long for both to decide to head back to Kansas City.

Things were not much happier at WDAF where John's brief successor was having trouble adjusting to the job, and the audience (and top station management) were having trouble adjusting to him.

Chapter 21

BACK IN KANSAS CITY

ONE MORNING IN SEPTEMBER, with no advance warning, John walked into the newsroom and flopped down in a chair and said: "I want my old job back.

Top management at the station had changed. A new general manager was brought in just before John left. The decision to hire him back took just a few minutes. John had been gone less than 90 days.

He was back on the job in another day with only one difference. He was strictly in traffic, and except in rare cases involving huge emergencies, he left the news coverage to the news staff.

Being removed from the news department and being reassigned as a personality reporting traffic for the program department meant a new freedom for John. There are certain things newsmen may not say, may not do. There are certain places newsmen may not go, for obvious reasons. A newsman should NEVER do commercials, should never recommend a commercial product, should never take part in grand openings or entertainment events on shopping center parking lots. But it is permissible for a station personality to make such appearances.

This left John free to make certain observations in traffic situations such as car chases. He never could have been allowed to say such things had he been a member of the news department.

He loved car chases and elevated their coverage to an art

form. He loved being directly overhead as some driver tried to outrun the police for any reason. John's philosophy was, "A driver is innocent until he runs. Then he's fair game."

It was always best when the fleeing driver was a full-fledged criminal — a bank robber, a rapist, a child molester, a burglar. But even if he was only a traffic offender, that was good enough. He shouldn't run from police ... or John Wagner.

John was not sympathetic to those offenders. On the radio he called them suckers, someone not quite bright, and he pursued them in and on the air with the same verbal enthusiasm as the police chased them physically on the ground.

John's car chase descriptions were the stuff of local legend. The police quickly caught on and tuned police car radios automatically to WDAF when a chase began. They knew that they had not only a friend in the air, but a fellow who would give them fresher and more detailed information than their dispatchers could provide. He made himself part of their team, and except for a few who considered themselves Wehrmacht rather than Kansas City Police, most officers welcomed John's assistance. They even admired it.

John's aggressiveness was bound to ruffle some feathers. He was prone to be heavy-handed with the advice, whether to pursuing police or to drivers who were trying to get to work or get home. He had little use for a multitude of tow-truck drivers who used their police scanners or listened to WDAF to get accident locations and get there ahead of ambulances and police cars. John was sharply critical of one such driver one day on the WDAF two-way radio system, but not on the main radio station. The furious hook driver called the radio station and urged that John be ordered to fly a little lower so he could get a good shot at him with a shotgun. John's work did produce emotional response. His many years of covering traffic gave John a proprietary feeling. It was HIS traffic, and they were HIS streets. Or so it seemed to his listeners. And he seemed especially offended when some traffic violator tried to outrun police. After all, the police were trying to keep order on John's thoroughfares.

One memorable day a motorcyclist, operating way above the posted speed limit, headed into Kansas City from Independence, with half the Independence Police Department in hot pursuit.

From his vantage point, John could see the procession and watched Kansas City Police set up barricades to try to stop the speeder. WDAF listeners heard John say that the cyclist veered around the roadblocks, got as far as Prospect, suddenly turned and headed back toward his pursuers.

John was peppering the air with suggestions for stopping the machine, including urging police to re-close the violated barricades. One policeman, obviously hearing John on the radio, got his cruiser in place just in time for the police car to be hit by the motorcycle.

Wagner told his audience how the motorcyclist flew through the air, going at least a hundred feet and landing on his head. John assumed the man was dead and reported he was being loaded into an ambulance. Later that day John learned the man had suffered (thanks to his helmet) only minor injury and was released — not by police — but by the hospital. For all the trouble he caused, the traffic violator (and his helmet) went to jail.

In such exciting moments, WDAF's disc jockeys (usually) would stop what they were doing and turn the radio station over to John in the airplane. They did it that day and allowed listeners to hear a very dramatic story as it unfolded. It was great radio broadcasting and was also a service to the public. The message: stay out of the way!

In reporting traffic he was allowed to let his pro-police and anti-traffic offender bias out in public view and hearing. He would not have been allowed that luxury had he still been a member of the news department.

Despite Wagner's hard-line approach to traffic violators, there were some exceptions. In late afternoon one day, a time called drive-time, what appeared to be a traffic violator was operating very dangerously in heavy afternoon traffic on I-435 on Kansas City's far east side. The car, driven by a middle-aged woman going north, had already brushed a couple of cars and a truck. John quickly became aware of the situation and flew directly over the car. He warned people on I-435 that this was dangerous. The car was weaving all over the road. He watched it hit several more cars without stopping. Ordinarily such flagrant driving would have drawn John's wrath. But something was wrong here. Something kept him from blasting away at the driver. Compassion seemed the better course.

Still the car headed north, and no police car was in sight. This left the situation temporarily in the hands of Officer Wagner. He began calling any police car in the area to get over to I-435 right away and corral the driver. Then, as he continued to warn other drivers out ahead of the weaving car, John saw a police car get into line behind the offending car and reported its driver was ignoring the red lights and siren. Suddenly the car rolled into the median trip and slowed down. Still it kept moving. The policeman could not get to the car on foot because it was still rolling. Then it stopped, and the officer was able to reach into the car and get the keys.

Then the wisdom of Wagner's compassionate approach to the story was clear. The policeman radioed for emergency medical assistance for the woman. She was having some serious problems and was about to go into a diabetic coma. She was treated not as a traffic violator, but as a seriously ill woman who needed help in a hurry. She was treated that way not only by the police officer, but also by John who then began ordering drivers to get out of the way, quit gawking and clear a path for the ambulance.

He could be a nice guy when the occasion required it. Wagner's displays of compassion were reserved strictly for those occasions that really required them. They were not heard daily.

Since John started in the broadcasting business back in Wichita, he had been an inventor (or re-inventor) of words. Many of them were applied to those who made mistakes in driving. He seldom gave benefit of the doubt to a hapless soul whose car stalled on Ward Parkway. The immediate Wagner conclusion: "a rich Johnson County driver who didn't have sense enough to keep his gas tank filled."

Others he called "Nimrods, Klutzheimers, Wizards of Sky Spyry, My Fellow I-70ers, and other terms of derision. His Klutzheimer attracted the greatest public attention. Several listeners wrote him. One even set up a Klutzheimer organization and sent John a petition signed by all its "charter" members.

His list included somewhat caustic advice: "Get your head on a swivel (in other words, look in all directions); hang a light on that heap (turn on your car lights); pull it over and park it. We'll build a garage over it; streets are made to move traffic — not park it." He formed an organization calling itself W I M P S, an acronym for We Irritate Motorists on Public Streets.

A particularly uncooperative police department was characterized as a "one antenna police department." And its city was referred to as "The People's Republic of Kansas City, Kansas; Raytown; Independence," or some other city whose police department chose to forget that the public DOES have a right to know what is going on. From John Wagner they got all the consideration they earned, which in many cases was very little.

On the other hand, praise for all involved came from John the morning a school bus was involved in a collision on busy I-470 in the far southeast part of the city. John was above the crash scene in the airplane and was in radio contact with John Chamberlain who served a local car agency as its "Rescue Ranger." Working in concert with Wagner, Chamberlain would rush to the scene of a reported breakdown or accident and render mechanical assistance and even more.

This incident required far more than just mechanical help. A man's life was in serious danger. The children were off the school bus, but the driver was in serious trouble. The crash had mangled the front end of the bus, trapping the driver in his seat. Then fire broke out.

Chamberlain went aboard the bus to try to free the driver and fight the fire with his own extinguisher. It quickly ran out. John Wagner, above, called for more help. "You truckers all carry fire extinguishers. I can see many of your rigs on this very highway. If you can't stop and help, at least toss your extinguisher out as you drive by, so someone else can use it."

In no time at all, a pile of fire extinguishers accumulated near the bus, and Chamberlain was relieved to see the Kansas City Fire Department arriving. Together they got the driver out and on his way to a hospital.

Then as tow truck crews began to move the wrecked bus and others off the highway, John Wagner took a moment to summarize all that had happened in the previous few minutes. He reconstructed the accident, listed the sequence of events, noted the drama of it, and thanked all involved. It was typical of Wagner's ability to put everything into perspective. He finished with these words: "In short, there were many heroes down there this morning. I can't count all of them. I can't even name them. But they know who they are, and they should be feeling pretty good. This is John Wagner — Sky Spy Overhead."

John always appreciated and recognized real heroes. These were the people who went the extra mile, sometimes at their own peril, to help someone who was in real trouble. This most often applied to a policeman or a fireman.

He could be just as vocal in the other direction when he suspected pomposity. One man in line for the Wagner treatment was a high-ranking police commander who had the bearing of a field marshal. He was harsh on the officers who ignored some of the petty rules, such as never being seen in public or in news photos not wearing a police hat. Reprimands and other punishment followed.

John's friends on the force kept him abreast of all that was happening. So it was inevitable that some of that information found its way into John's traffic reports. At the end of one particularly tough police chase, John commented on the air: "It's all over now. Police have the bad guy in custody. They stopped him before he killed anyone. And all of them wore their hats. That'll make Headquarters happy."

He also had little use for panic or fear. On days when the weather forecast included snow or ice (which hadn't yet developed), he noticed that some drivers were, in his view, a little too cautious, he sternly lectured, "Drive the conditions — not the forecast."

One day the call everyone dreads came. John's father Leslie was near death in Chicago. Their estrangement was so serious John was reluctant to pay him a final visit. But he did, and he was glad he went. A few days later the final call came, and John headed back to Chicago to bury his dad. John and Helen were alone at the service. The body was cremated, and the remains were given to John. He planned to bury the remains the next day, but that night he and Helen went to dinner. As they drove up to the Black Angus on Western Avenue, John remarked, "This is the first time I ever took my dad to dinner, and he's in the trunk."

The next day John drove to the cemetery lot owned by his dad and urged a man driving a small truck with auger attached to bore a small hole on the gravesite. John placed the remains in the hole, filled it in, took one last look around and returned to Kansas City, where more battles remained to be fought.

Kansas City human nature had not changed in the few days John was in Chicago. John was flying afternoon traffic and heard the excited shouts of policemen on his radio. This meant another high-speed chase. The speeding car was running south on I-29 from Platte City. John always believed that people who run from police are not smart. And this was further proof. If one really wants to get away, he should go away from a city and not toward it. But that's what he did.

The old veteran traffic reporter was in perfect form that day. In rapid-fire fashion he warned drivers in the area and gave police instructions on how to catch the violator. As the chase neared Kansas City, many local police cars joined the caravan. There were already city, county and state police cars headed at top speed toward the Paseo Bridge.

Suddenly the speeder turned east on Highway 210 in

North Kansas City. Wagner's airplane was directly over the offending car. Again he warned other drivers to stay out of the way and gave police more of his best advice on how to surround and stop the car.

One way was to form a box around the car, a tricky and dangerous maneuver at high speed. It ran back and forth with the speeder seeming to have all the luck, but then the boxing-in maneuver fell into place, and the car was stopped. All the while John was broadcasting on WDAF.

The driver got out and ran a short distance, but some young, healthy police officers made it a very short foot chase.

John's description of that one was very exciting, especially since the stall alarm in the airplane cockpit could be heard on the air. This was an indication he was flying back and forth, making sudden turns and dives, and was briefly, but still losing air speed. Later, when asked if he had been flying too low, John said, "I may have left a few landing gear tire marks on his hood."

Wagner's broadcast reports always produced an emotional response from the public. Some, usually the targets of his barbs, didn't like him and said so. Others admired his gutsy, daring approach and said so. Those who liked and admired John's work greatly outnumbered those who did not.

This writer had to referee several disagreements between John and some law enforcement agencies. Once when approaching a plane crash at the old State Line Airport in far south Kansas City, this writer was approached by a Kansas State Highway Patrol trooper who asked, "Are you John Wagner?" After getting a denial, the trooper said, "Well, John Wagner is the best trooper we've got." (whew!)

His remaining years at WDAF were marked by more car chases, more major fires, more train wrecks (which can be seen best and reported from the air), more confrontations over his critical remarks and more excitement, along with more frustration.

He was particularly good at covering aircraft accidents, because he understood flying so well. These included the crash of an airplane into the Telephone Building at 11th and Oak (years earlier), the crash landing of a small plane near the 12th Street viaduct in the west bottoms, and the crash of a big four-engine Lockheed Electra loaded with auto parts between 7th Street and the Fairfax Bridge.

Early the morning of November 30, 1988, John nosed his airplane toward Blue River Road and 71 Highway, where an hour earlier six firemen, two entire engine companies, were killed in an explosion. Many tons of ammonium nitrate blew up as the unsuspecting crews of Pumpers 30 and 41 fought what seemed to be a routine fire.

The area was sealed off by police as a "crime scene." John flew over it and joined other WDAF newsmen in the station's coverage of the tragedy. Then someone said on the Fire Department radio frequency, "Call the control tower and tell them to keep all aircraft out of here." John was broadcasting on WDAF at the moment, high above the blast site. He heard the remark and commented on the air, "What you want is not necessarily what you are going to get." In other words, "I'm staying here."

John's remark was ill advised, but not as ill advised as the request to keep aircraft away. Nonetheless, some people thought John was interfering with the investigation and the retrieval of bodies of victims. That was nonsense. John was doing his job and was not interfering with anything. He didn't get much backing from the radio station in that matter. And it was an indication to John that he would eventually be heading into another career crisis.

His relationship with a disc jockey program director began to disintegrate, and by spring of 1990 his contract with WDAF had expired and negotiations seemed to be going nowhere.

Chapter 22

MORE CHANGES AHEAD

IN JANUARY 1991, seven months later, John was contacted by a rival "traffic reporting service" and accepted an offer to leave WDAF. This turned out to be a mistake, but staying at WDAF would have been an equally serious mistake.

His working life had come to resemble a large dramatic production with a great number of entrances and exits. He left WDAF, where despite professions of grief over losing him, a "replacement" seemed ready to step into the job immediately, as though pre-planned.

The new job was not a good one and was destined to be short. The first problem was John's attempt to use the term "Sky Spy." He didn't realize it, but WDAF legally owned the name and went to court to block John's use of it. This left him to find some other title, and by court order it could not resemble or rhyme with Sky Spy.

Then came some maintenance problems with the airplane the new employer provided. Next the radio station using John's services was a strictly disc jockey operation, with no feeling whatever for the serious parts of the business, news, traffic safety, emergency situations. All that mattered was not taking too much time away from the stars, the disc jockeys. To complicate the picture further, two paychecks issued to John bounced.

But all of those concerns became moot on May 15, 1991, when John was forced to make a dead-stick (no power) landing in a grassy field on church school property on Red Bridge Road. The engine quit, as they always do when they don't get gasoline.

Regardless of who was responsible for filling the gas tanks on the airplane, the blame falls squarely on the pilot's shoulders. Add that deadly serious problem to the acrobatic maneuvers for which John was already convicted, and you have a flying career in serious peril. Someone said God will forgive sin, but the FAA will not. It was the end of Wagner's flying career.

Now grounded, he spent several months selling recreation vehicles for a dealer on I-35, but found little satisfaction. He realized that he was truly sick of city living. He had spent his entire life on the streets and sidewalks of Chicago, Wichita and Kansas City. It was no longer fun. John needed a total change of environment.

He remembered boyhood vacation trips from Chicago to a relative's farm in Wisconsin. The memory was pleasant. He realized rural Missouri is nice, too. He and Helen took a number of trips to the countryside, and on a fateful visit they were totally unprepared to make a deal. He left his checkbook at home in Kansas City. The initial agreement had to be strictly verbal. It worked.

The house in Kansas City was sold, and John and Helen moved to a five-acre spread in Hickory County, Missouri. The previous owner was a Japanese "war bride" who was an outstanding gardener. John has expanded her gardens and now grows a wide variety of flowers and vegetables.

Hearing aids in both ears indicate the hours spent flying and wearing headphones. His pilot's logbook shows 13,000 hours, which translates easily to a million miles flown mostly in a control zone.

The man who was once a "child of the pavement" in big cities now lives on a gravel road, a mile and a half from the nearest pavement. He doesn't hear sirens or gunfire often. Instead, he hears birds, coyotes and other sounds of nature.

He still has that emergency radio scanner in the kitchen,

mostly to pick up weather and rural fire information "just to keep in touch." He is far from the mean streets of Kansas City and enjoys his new life.

He can look back with satisfaction on an interesting career, a career that can never happen again. The broadcasting business wouldn't tolerate a free-wheeling "Lone Ranger" which he surely was. And officialdom wouldn't tolerate it either. Police can't imagine allowing someone they can't control to get near anything resembling news. After all, the public might find out what is happening. And even worse with a man such as John Wagner getting too close, police might lose all control of what is reported and photographed. Big Brother wouldn't approve.

John Wagner's years of Kansas City broadcast news and traffic reporting made up a Golden Age. What is broadcast today is a poor substitute. The broadcast reporters today are surely nice people, kind to children, gentle to dogs and fit well in a world dominated by disc jockey mentality. But when they are compared to John Wagner as broadcast newsmen or traffic reporters, they have no significance.

It's a long and twisting path from the sidewalks of Chicago to the final months of World War Two on Pacific islands, to furniture and appliance stores, a laundry and a radio station in Wichita, to Kansas City, to the Virgin Islands and back to Kansas City, and finally to Hickory County, Missouri. It has been quite a journey. Some history was made along the way. And what a story it is.

All that said, the Wagner era in Kansas City broadcasting is over, and that's too bad. Life here hasn't been very interesting since he and Helen moved to the country.

'Sky Spy' Wagner leaves the air

It seemed like the perfect marriage last January when John Wagner, known to hundreds of thousands as WDAF-AM's "Sky Spy," signed on with the traffic reporting company operated by Johnny Rowlands, another radio veteran.

The union ended earlier this month when each man decided he had had enough. Now the 63-year-old Wagner is off the air, more than likely for good. Rowlands, meanwhile, says he is glad Wagner has retired.

"The last seven months have been the worst in my career," Wagner said. "The biggest mistake I ever made was being involved with Johnny Rowlands."

Rowlands said: "I regret that he feels the way he does, but I'm not surprised. John's reputation, at this point, is legendary as far as being difficult to please and hard to work with."

Wagner had patroled the skies

BARRY GARRON

for 61 Country since 1974, but in 1990 he felt unappreciated. He jumped at the chance to return to the pilot's seat and provide traffic updates for country competitor KFKF-FM.

For Rowlands, the move meant adding highly rated KFKF to his list of client stations. And KFKF was delighted to welcome one of the most recognized personalities in local radio.

"It was one of those things that looked great going in," Rowlands said. "I told John when I hired him that I wanted him to be able to look back on this as the best move he ever made."

For about four months that seemed possible. But things started to unravel after Wagner made an emergency landing May 14.

The Federal Aviation Administration has not completed its investigation, but Rowlands and Wagner agree the landing was forced when Wagner's plane ran out of fuel as it circled the metropolitan area.

Wagner said the incident had little to do with his leaving Airborne Traffic. He said there were other problems, such as getting two payroll checks returned for insufficient funds.

Wagner also said he was forced to fly in an ill-equipped aircraft that was too small for two people. "We needed an AM-FM radio in the airplane. I was using a Walkman to pick up my cues," Wagner said.

Also, Wagner said, "we had exactly one pound to play with to keep from being over the gross weight limit."

Rowlands said the two bounced paychecks were caused by a mixup when accounts were changed. "As soon as the problem was identified, he got his money," Rowlands said.

It was Wagner's choice to use a Walkman, he added, because the plane had a radio.

Rowlands also said the Cessna 152 in which Wagner rode was a training aircraft that routinely flies at the gross weight limit. "For a guy who flew practically without fuel for 1½ hours, it seems a little ludicrous to me that he would worry about the gross weight limit."

After the May 14 landing, Rowlands thought he could not permit Wagner to pilot a company-rented airplane. Rowlands worried that the incident, which might have endangered the public, would reflect poorly on his company.

"I don't think that John could ever quite grasp the impact of what happened to me from a business and a personal standpoint," Rowlands said.

The one point on which Wagner and Rowlands agreed was to praise KFKF for its handling of the situation.

"If it had not been for [general manager] Dan Wastler and [program director] Dean James and the staff over there, I would have quit a lot sooner," Wagner said.

Rowlands said: "If there's any ray of sunshine in this, it's that I had the opportunity to work with them."